LEABHARLANNA CHONTAE FHINE GALL
FINGAL COUNTY LIBRARIES

Blanchardstown Library
Tel: 8905560

Items should be returned on or before the last date shown below.
Items may be renewed by personal application, writing, telephone
or by accessing the online Catalogue Service on Fingal Libraries'
website. To renew give date due, borrower ticket number and PIN
number if using online catalogue. Fines are charged on overdue
items and will include postage incurred in recovery. Damage to, or
loss of items will be charged to the borrower.

Date Due	Date Due	Date Due
04. OCT 07.	10. APR	
04. OCT 07.	21. APR 08.	
17. OCT 07.	12.	
23. NOV	21. MAY 08	
22. JAN 08	18. JUN 08	
30. JAN 08		
23. FEB 08		
27. MAR 08		

Tell Me Why, Mummy

Tell Me Why, Mummy

A little boy's struggle to survive
A mother's shameful secret

DAVID THOMAS

HarperElement
An Imprint of HarperCollins*Publishers*
77-85 Fulham Palace Road,
Hammersmith, London W6 8JB

The website address is: www.thorsonselement.com

and *HarperElement* are trademarks of
HarperCollins*Publishers* Ltd

First published by HarperElement 2007

1 3 5 7 9 10 8 6 4 2

A catalogue record of this book is
available from the British Library

ISBN-13 978-0-00-725543-6 (hardback)
ISBN-10 0-00-725543-8 (hardback)
ISBN-13 978-0-00-725544-3 (paperback)
ISBN-10 0-00-725544-6 (paperback)

Printed and bound in Great Britain by
Clays Ltd, St Ives plc

Mixed Sources
Product group from well-managed
forests and other controlled sources
www.fsc.org   Cert no. SW-COC-1806
© 1996 Forest Stewardship Council

To my children Molly, Nathan, and Danielle
who have shown me the greatest pleasure
of all is being a parent

Disclaimer

Tell My Why, Mummy is a true story – it's my true story. All the people and events described in this book are real, but to protect the privacy of my family and others, all names apart from mine have been changed. However, the descriptions are based on real people and similarly the names of locations have been changed to fictitious locations although the descriptions are based on real places.

Halifax in West Yorkshire, of course, is a real town – it is my home town.

David Thomas
Halifax, May 2007

Prologue

I know she has been drinking again. I can hear her crashing around upstairs and then, suddenly, she's in the kitchen. She can barely stand as she staggers through the door and gropes her way along the grubby kitchen cabinets, trying to get to me across the room.

I'm playing with my bricks on the lino floor. She starts tottering towards me, falls over, and then tries to lie down next to me. She is completely naked, her eyes glazed and unfocused as she emits a low drunken moan.

'David,' she says, her voice alternating between an inaudible moan and a loud drunken shout, 'come over here.'

She doesn't seem to realize that I am already close beside her. When she tells me to do something I always do it at once. I love to please her and I hate to displease her. If I don't do as I'm told she may stop loving me. She won't smack me or hurt me, but I think she will be angry. So I stand up and then sit down again, so that she can see that I am there, next to her.

When she sees me near her, she looks up and pulls me down towards her. She then takes my hand and places it between her legs, which are spread wide open. It feels strange and I don't understand why she's doing this. She rubs my hand up and down between her legs and starts to moan again. She is sighing and keeps moving my hand inside her and then — I don't know why or how — I start to realize that the loud moaning noises are not, as I first thought, signs of distress but of pleasure.

As this dawns on me, and because she continues to moan, I take it that this game is good and so I'm happy to continue to do it as long as she wants to. She carries on rubbing herself with my hand for some time until she has had enough.

Then she pushes my hand away and without saying a word, my mother picks up her bottle and staggers back across the kitchen to make her way upstairs, while I go back to playing with my bricks on the lino floor.

PART 1

The Chosen One

1

Living in the Shadows

Most of the time you're the best Mummy in the whole world. But then you change. You get angry and make me do things I don't understand. Why do you want me do those things? Please tell me why. Why can't you make my dark Mummy go away? I'm afraid of her. Don't you see what she does? Don't you see what she makes me do? Why do you pretend you don't know?

I am only five but I've already got so many questions I can feel them pressing on my heart. Sometimes it's hard to breathe. There aren't any answers, just more questions. I don't know if I will ever have the answers. All I know is that my questions are piling up inside me. I try to bury them but there are too many. I feel like an unexploded mine.

* * *

The house in which I am born, on 6 April 1968, is in an idyllic setting: the small rural village of Calder Bridge, near Halifax in West Yorkshire. The village is picture-postcard perfect with beautiful cottages made from

Yorkshire stone, a small village pub and post office, all wrapped up in the incredible rolling landscape of the Pennine Hills. I love the glorious countryside feel to it – the large wide-open spaces, the rolling fields, the luscious woodland, the sense of freedom. Even aged three or four, my mother lets me wander through the woods to play with other kids. Everyone knows everyone else and there's a real sense of community.

Our house is quite isolated though. It stands in a fork in a country lane and is one of four terraced charcoal-grey-stone cottages, smothered at each end with dark-green ivy, surrounded by trees and perched above a steep ravine through which a sparkling river runs over mossy rocks and boulders. Although from the front of the building the cottages seem squat, with small, poky rooms where the light never spreads, the back of the building slopes steeply down towards the ravine. So there are only two floors on the front of house, but two more floors at the back. They tower over the river, and even in summer the whole building is gloomy and mysterious like a gothic mansion.

My earliest memories are of these strange contrasts – the warm, cosy, intimate times when I play with my mother; the cold, isolated, dark, forbidding times when things are completely different – in my family life as well as in the places surrounding it.

Years ago, there was a cotton mill a hundred yards along the ravine and you can still see signs of it along the brick banks of the river. A hundred yards from my home, between where the mill used to be and the house, is an old scrap-metal yard which may very well be the most beautiful scrapyard in the world, as it virtually hangs over the river.

The scrapyard is a second home to me. I love looking up at all this wonderful metal piled up as far as I can see. It's dirty and greasy, a perfect place for a small boy. I play hide and seek with the owner's young son Jeff, in and around the stacks of rubber tyres, dustbins, stripped doors, racks of trellises, lead piping, stained and damaged cast-iron baths and wash basins, wrecked car parts, and all the other layers of junk that have settled one on top of the other like geological strata in this metal wonderland. Jeff's father is gruff but kindly, a good-humoured, plain-speaking Yorkshireman who sometimes smiles but never says much to me.

When I'm not playing with Jeff, I play by myself or sometimes with George, a lad of my age who lives a few fields away, and whose mother gets on well with mine. My earliest memories are of forever playing outside. Although as a young child I am not very adventurous or physically courageous, I am naturally inquisitive and am always look-ing for birds and animals in the fields and fish in the river.

One day, playing in the scrapyard, I find a bird's nest, embedded deep within some rusty metal boulders. Even as a four-year-old I am amazed at how tough, tenacious and adaptable life is; how such a vulnerable thing as a bird's nest with its firm outer ring and its gentle cosy lining can find a home in this alien place; how life can grow and thrive here, in the shadows.

The next time I go to see the nest, the chicks have hatched. I stare at the broken shells in amazement. Only yesterday they were tiny fragile pear-shaped eggs with beautiful, delicate patterns. When I return later in the day all the shells have gone.

I ask the scrapyard owner what's happened to them.

'Mother's eaten 'em, lad, or chucked 'em away,' he says. 'She like to keeps things clean and tidy.'

'I liked the eggs,' I say.

'Aye lad, but as they always say, you can't make an omelette without breaking eggs.'

I think about this Omlet and wonder how many eggs you must break to make it. Are all the chicks baby Omlets and what happens to the mother Omlet? Do they all stay in the nest together or do they fly away and never see each other again?

I go down to the nest every day after that and look at the chicks.

One day when I go to the nest, I find it empty. I wonder what's happened to the chicks and where they've gone. I think they must have all turned into Omlets and flown away.

Dad has a lock-up garage near the scrapyard where he stores something special. One day he shows me what he keeps inside: it's a red Volvo P1800. I'm very excited as this is the car used by Simon Templar in the TV show *The Saint*. The Volvo is impossibly beautiful with swooping curves and looks very exotic – as good as any other car on the road. We also have a Rover called Bluebell which Dad keeps on a patch of grass on the side of the house. It's a gorgeous car – the kind Jim Callaghan drives and Mum says he's a very important man and one day he might even be Prime Minister.

My father, Keith, is a big man, a foot taller than my mother, with a large face, horn-rimmed glasses, short black hair combed back from his forehead and a thick black beard. He doesn't have a moustache though, so when I'm older I think his beard looks like one of those joke beards you stick on your chin to make you look like a monkey or a rabbi.

He likes making jokes, my Dad, but in other ways he can be a bit of a cold fish — he's not affectionate with me and there's never any rough and tumble with him. He is genial and patient towards me but he's also strict — firm but fair. Unlike my mother, he isn't sociable or gregarious. He doesn't smile a whole lot.

Dad works as a draughtsman but his true obsession is his motorbikes and engines. We have lots of space in the house and he even has a garage underneath the house just for his motorbikes, which he rides up and down the lane. He may not have built this garage himself but he's changed it to make it the way he wants it to be. Down in the garage, I peer up at him in wonder as he takes apart the engine. He lets me watch and answers my questions.

'What you doing, Dad?'

'I'm just changing the oil in the gearbox.'

'Why, Dad?'

'To keep the gears all working nicely, son.'

'How d'you do it?'

'Well, you have to remove the drain plug from the gearbox, drain the oil, and then remove the gearbox fill plug and fill it with new oil. Then you wipe away any oil you've spilt so it's all clean and replace the chassis protector ...'

And on he goes, carefully explaining what he's doing. I don't really understand what he's saying though. After changing the oil, he'll start on the nuts and bolts.

'Can I help you, Dad?'

'Yes, you can hand me that spanner, lad.'

'What's that for?'

'Just to tighten the nuts around these bolts ... look. But you mustn't screw them too tight. Otherwise you'll never be able to loosen them if you need to. Gently does it.'

I watch as he tightens the nuts, totally lost in what he's doing. After that, he polishes all the chrome until it shines like the sun gleaming over the river.

The house we live in is one of a row of four. As the other three come up for sale Dad buys them all. The odd thing is, though, that I know some of the other houses are, or used to, owned by my Mum's family. Is my Dad getting richer while my Mum's family are getting poorer? These things are mysteries to me. I may never know the truth.

Our house above the river is our little patch of heaven. We have no direct neighbours, but there's a farmer up the road who stops and talk as he passes our house many times a day. Although we eventually own all four houses, the really strange thing is that we only live in one, which always feels dark inside. That's because it's overshadowed by trees and also because the rooms are small and the windows let in very little light.

The house is bare and simply furnished; the kitchen has very basic chipboard cupboards and lino on the floor. I've seen lino in other people's kitchens so we're not that different from other people, at least as far as that goes. But I think about the kitchen lino for another, much stranger reason.

* * *

My parents met through the Methodist Church. They were in the choir and, as my mother is always keen to point out, both were as innocent as young lambs when they married in 1966. But as far as I know, from the brief times I spend in George's house with his family and then when I look at my Mum and Dad and me, I can already see that we don't seem to work like a normal family – we never do things together. I spend time just with Dad and his cars and bikes, or I spend time just with Mum, who can be great fun when she wants to be.

Mum's name before she was married to my Dad was Carol Stones and she was born in March 1945. There's a photo of her as a little girl with her older brother Jim in a big dark wooden frame in the living room: she's smiling straight at me, looking very sweet with a cheeky grin. Jim's much taller, with darker hair. There are other photos of Mum: in one she's holding her doll and looks like a mummy dolly holding her baby dolly – they've both got the same curly golden hair. In another photo her hair is much straighter, like pale straw, and she's got plaits and is standing with other children in her class; in others she's swimming in the sea; riding a donkey; walking with her dog; in yet another photo she looks like a fairy princess with a bunch of roses and silver crown – I think she's a bridesmaid but I don't know who the bride is.

In all these photos Mum has the same round face, chubby cheeks and mischievous look. As my Grandad, her dad, would say, 'When she was a lass she was a smasher.'

There's another photo in a lighter plastic frame. She's older in this one and has turned into a strawberry-blonde teenager. She's smiling at me again and her smile is warm and friendly. In another photo she's a grown-up woman – I think she's a bridesmaid again – and her hair is piled on top of her head with a light-blue ribbon the same colour as her dress and she's wearing white shoes with pointed toes. There's a also a grey-looking photo of Mum in nurse's uniform only in this one she's not smiling.

There are also photos of Mum and Dad's wedding at the Methodist church. She's all in white and he's all in black. Her face is less plump in these pictures and she looks different — softer and more frail — but very happy. Dad's grinning, like he's just eaten the cherry on the cake.

There's one other photo of Mum and Dad together that I love to look at. They're at the zoo together and are both laughing like they're having fun. Dad's wearing his black shiny PVC Pacamac and has one arm round Mum. Tucked under his other arm is a tiny black monkey. Mum's holding her free arm out. Perched on her elbow is a large parrot who's gazing inquisitively at both of them. I like to think that they've had at least a few good times together.

Later, in my teenage years it dawns on me that when I was a child Mum was always slightly unkempt, never very well dressed; her hair a little scruffy; she wasn't beautiful but she had good skin (and freckles) and was still attractive. By the time I turned up she had adopted a tight perm which she kept throughout her life. She never wore much make-up and, as she grew older, her dress sense seemed to disappear almost completely. But when she was happy, she had a great smile and an infectious laugh.

My mum was 23 when I was born. She never talks about her early childhood with her brother and parents, but occasionally mentions small things about her teenage years, such as how she once went on a motorbike with a boyfriend which she thought was very exciting.

As early as I can remember I visit other local houses with her and we often go for walks in the woods. She likes to show me all the flowers and we pick them together. She is warm and affectionate to me, and sociable to others. My dad is also sociable, though not in such a warm way. Mum has a good sense of humour – as long as she doesn't feel she's having the mickey taken out of her. She can never handle that very well.

Other people always respond to Mum. She can strike up a conversation with a lamp-post and has a way of getting people to talk about themselves quite quickly. They feel they can open up to her and she has a few solid, long-term friends. She will chat away for hours and hours about personal things – about people she knows and what's happening in their life and their problems – and what she's saying about them is as much a mystery to me as when Dad talks about his bikes and his engines.

But my mother's life and personality are made up of two separate halves: she is two different people. She is loving, caring, affectionate and supportive, and can be funny, sympathetic and always keen to talk.

But she also has a dark side and when it surfaces it is a bad place to be – not just for her but also for me when I am with her. It's not just bad, it's dreadful. She turns into another person: nasty, spiteful, vindictive, malicious, uncaring, inconsiderate. Mummy normally never says bad words and thinks it's dreadfully rude to fart or burp – but when she's in the dreadful place she uses lots of bad words.

When I am very little the bad words themselves don't mean anything to me, but the effect of them, and the way she hurls them at me – or at the walls and furniture as she slams and barges into them – is very, very frightening.

I sense this has a lot to do with my Mummy drinking because I've seen her drink a lot of foul-smelling liquid which I've found out is called brandy. She drinks it very, very quickly until she is almost asleep. Except that she's not asleep. She's still awake and that's when she scares me.

The brandy on its own is bad enough but there's worse to come. When she gets drunk she will come and find me and press her body on me. The memory of the first time my Mummy does this stays with me for the rest of my life, even though I'm still only four years old.

* * *

She has been drinking as usual and even at this early age I can sense that she's out of control as she orders me to play with her on the kitchen lino.

Without having any idea what is really going on, or why she's in the state she's in, I know that she's not the same person who walks with me in the woods and it terrifies me. As her face moves towards me I can smell the strong, acrid odour on her breath. Her movements, as she lurches across me, are clumsy and out of control. I just want this Mummy to go away and for my good Mummy to come back, but I know that isn't going to happen when she takes my hand and places it between her legs.

She is rubbing my hand up and down, up and down, between her legs, against this soft, hairy thing that she calls her minnie. Caught in my fear, I am anxious, desperate even, to please her. I am looking for the slightest signs that I can make Mum happy, to stop the raging anger in her. I continue to rub my hand up and down her minnie until, finally, she pushes it away.

To my relief, she has calmed down and somehow I know I must have been doing the right thing: she has stopped acting strangely now and it's me who made her feel better. I feel a strange sense of triumph, of achievement. I feel that she needs me and that I can make the bad things go away for her.

I am still frightened but I also feel proud that I have been singled out: my Mummy has asked me to play a game with her and I am the chosen one to do it.

* * *

This morning, Mum and Dad are having an argument. Dad's often away travelling nowadays and even when he's at home, he's not really there. They never spend much time together and when they do, they don't seem to be happy.

Dad never gets angry or loses his temper and this morning, right in the middle of this very bad row, he is sitting calmly in the front room drinking his coffee. I don't know whether Mum is drunk or not but she's very angry and she's getting more upset by the second. She's shrieking at Dad and throwing things and I have no idea what he's done and I even wonder whether he does.

I wish they'd stop but I don't think they even know I'm there. Suddenly she gets up and throws her cup of coffee all over him. He gets up without a word and walks out of the room and out of the house.

* * *

I am growing more aware of Mum's drinking. When she drinks I can sense a huge rage in her and I'm starting to see how bad it is for Dad to live with her because I know what it's like to be in a room with her when she turns into someone else – someone I'm afraid of.

As the days and weeks go on, Dad goes away on his business trips more and more, and I stop asking Mum when he's coming home.

Finally, one day, I know he won't be coming back ever again when Mum tells me that she and Dad can't live together any more and from now on it's just her and me.

'Why doesn't Dad want to live with us, Mummy?' I ask.

'He just doesn't, David,' she replies dully. I think maybe she's hoping I won't ask her again. She's making jam in the kitchen which is something she enjoys doing, but I sense that this morning she's doing it to keep busy and to stop herself from falling apart.

'But why? Tell me why, Mummy.'

'Because we're unhappy together, because ... *just don't keep asking*,' she snaps.

I know better than to ask again when she uses that tone. Instead I go off to the scrapyard and hide in the nooks and crannies of the metal caves, and think about my daddy who talks to me about his bikes and cars and sometimes cracks jokes which I don't always understand and who won't be coming home again.

I am starting to cry when I hear footsteps nearby.

'You there, Dave?' comes the voice of the scrapyard owner's son.

'Be right there, Jeff.'

I climb out of my hidey hole and go and play. My dad won't be back and there's no point in asking again.

But it turns out I'm wrong about Dad not coming back. Not only does he return to the house but he also remains in the house. It's Mum and me who move out – in fact we move exactly three houses away to the other end of the block of four terraced houses. Both houses feel very similar. They have the same sort of furniture, which is another way of saying that they are both pretty bare.

So there's Dad at one end of the block, and me and Mum at the other end. In the months to come I go from one house to the other, spending huge amounts of time with Mum but very little with Dad. He's often busy, usually away travelling, and he never seems to talk to me about anything personal to do with me and Mum or our wider family or our lives together. But he still chats easily about cars and bikes and things like that.

Every time I see him I long for a stronger bond between us, but it never happens. I wish he would cuddle me or sit me on his knee, but it hardly ever happens and it makes me feel sad.

* * *

My parents separate around 1973 when I am five but it isn't until many years later that Dad tells me that even though they both knew their marriage was over, it took some time for them to be able to sit down and talk it through because it could only be done when she wasn't drinking.

Even by the age of five there is a definite hole in my life developing. I am happy when Mum helps me to fill it by the way she pays me attention. She doesn't come to me and make me touch her every day – sometimes weeks go by without her coming to me in this way. But when she does, it somehow fulfils a need in us both.

She needs it for reasons that I am too young to understand. The reason for my need is much more simple: I need the attention. Even at this early age, it helps to build a bond between us. As she is now the only active parent I have, I instinctively understand the importance of this.

At the end of those times we spend together, when she wants me to touch her, she never thanks me but she doesn't tell me off either. That's to become the norm and that's how I want it to be.

I have always worked harder to avoid criticism than to chase praise.

I am too young to know that, in reality, my mother is taking advantage of my submissive nature, committing the worst abuse of the power she has over her child that any parent can. I will soon come to realize this, and that's when the problems really begin.

2

My Dark Mummy

In 1973 at the age of five I start school. Calder Bridge Primary School is a large old building with tall windows, built in the shade and surrounded by trees. Even in summer, it feels dark and cold, and looks like something out of a horror film. I am already a nervous child and I'm not looking forward to it.

To make matters worse, Mum takes me to school to begin with but then puts me on the bus. It's a short trip and she asks one of the older kids to look after me. Although Lizzie is a very nice girl I'm anxious about this arrangement and I can't understand why my mummy won't come with me on this bus and look after me.

'Please take me to school, Mum,' I plead as the bus comes round the corner.

'You'll be fine,' she says, putting me on the bus. 'Off you go.'

This isn't a good start for me at my new school and I feel lonely and insecure among all the strange faces. All the other children seem to have at least one parent taking them to school; some even have two.

I don't know anyone and I find it difficult to talk to the other children or make any friends. In my first year at

primary school I get picked on by a girl called Karen, two
or three years older than me.

She is tall and towers over me. I have ginger-red hair
and she soon discovers that I have a slight lisp and can't
pronounce my 's's clearly. After that she picks on me
mercilessly. I spend most of my time trying to avoid her
but she always manages to seek me out.

'What'th the matter, Ginger Bithcuit, have you done
poo-pooth in your troutherth?' she calls out to me in the
school playground. 'What'th your mummy going to thay?
I bet she'll thpank your bumbumth?'

'Go away! Leave me alone!' I reply miserably. 'I haven't
done anything to hurt you.'

'Oooh, baby Ginger Bithcuit'th cwying,' she taunts
back. 'He'th going to wee all over hith troutherth coth
he'th tho upthet. Boo hoo! Boo hoo! You'd better go and
tell your mummy and she can kith you better!'

I don't know how or why, but she's hit the target, picked
on my weak spot. I don't really understand what's going
on at home, but Mum scares me when she's out of control
and I somehow feel crushed and humiliated by this sneer-
ing jibe.

I blush bright scarlet.

'Look at Baby Ginger! Hith fathe hath gone all red. It'th
all gingery like the retht of him.'

Her friends laugh and snigger. But I'm praying that
she's had her fun now and if I'm lucky she'll leave me
alone now for the rest of the day. Of course she knows
very well that the last thing I'm going to do is tell Mum. I
can't tell my mother and I can't tell anyone else either.

Karen doesn't physically hurt me and I don't mention
these incidents to anyone, but this is the first time I have

been bullied and I hate it. It destroys my confidence and makes me deeply unhappy. I withdraw into myself, feeling that I'm on the outside looking in. From now on I keep myself to myself and mainly talk to the other quiet kids.

I'm not used to people being nasty to me like this. In the years to come I will come to understand that I have been bullied, just as I will come to realize that my mother has been sexually abusing me, but at the age of five I don't attach these labels to what is happening to me. All I know is that at school Karen makes my life miserable, while at home I have two mummies – the Light Mummy, the caring, loving and affectionate one, and the Dark Mummy, who frightens me when she's drinking and out of control.

But even with Dark Mummy, I can comfort myself that I'm doing to make her happy and if it pleases her it makes me feel better. Besides, she isn't hurting me and that's what matters.

I don't know if Mum notices the effect of the bullying on me, but after a few weeks I start inventing excuses for not going to school.

'I've got a headache/toothache/earache/my tummy/foot/elbow hurts.'

Usually Mum won't have any truck with these excuses: if I'm able to get up and eat my breakfast then I can go to school. Then, miraculously, I come down with a real stinker of a cold and sore throat and she keeps me at home for over a week.

When it's time for me to go back to school, I am more anxious and nervous than ever. But by this time, to my huge relief, Karen has grown bored with taunting me and apart from an occasional verbal swipe the bullying seems to tail off. Probably she has found another victim, but after that she leaves me alone.

Besides, things have started to change for me slightly. Maybe Karen has picked up on this and thinks twice before having a go at me, but for whatever reason, she has moved on and so have I.

What's changed is that I'm learning how to defend myself – and it helps that I wear clogs as shoes at school. There's a working clog factory a few miles from where we live and as they are sturdy and long-lasting, they seem not only practical but it also makes economic sense to Mum for me to wear them.

The front of a clog is very hard and hurts if you come into contact with it. Unfortunately, I choose to employ them as a weapon at school and start kicking out at any kid I fall out with. I have become physically aggressive to defend myself against being bullied.

This kicking out makes kids more wary of me. Upon kicking another pupil, they start screaming in pain and I find myself getting hauled up in front of the teacher. Despite my protests of doing it in self-defence, I get into trouble. As a rule I only tend to do it in the classroom and these incidents are few and far between, but I'm always unrepentant, which never helps.

'But Miss,' I plead, 'they were hitting me first.'

'I don't care, David,' she insists, 'you can't wear them any more.'

This scolding hurts me more than the bullying and I try to control myself. I also hate going home and telling Mum I have been in trouble at school.

It never occurs to me that there's anything very wrong with what's going on between me and Mum. I think of the peculiar physical intimacy between us as our 'Special Time' and I like it in the way that a child in a normal relationship with their mother is aware of and understands a cuddle. I don't want to spoil what we have between us, and so from now on I'm a model student at school, well behaved in class, hardly ever getting into detention and never being sent home from school.

After this I stop kicking out at other kids and I avoid conflicts. If someone tells me to do anything – whether it's grown-ups or other children – I agree to it or find a way round it to make sure that other people don't get angry or upset with me. I don't want to be hurt and I don't want to get into trouble for hurting anyone else. It's in my nature to be submissive and I don't want to be bullied – but that's going to lead to far greater problems for me in the years to come.

In my first year at Calder Bridge I win a gold star from the Head and I'm overjoyed. I've just discovered how much I like being the centre of attention. I enjoy the feeling of being good at something. When a few weeks later I see another older lad getting a lot of attention because it's his birthday it makes me feel very jealous. I wish it was me who they were all making a fuss about. I also discover something else.

Walking home from school with another boy, we race each other and I beat him.

I love beating him and I love winning.

*   *   *

At home, we have very little money to live on. After my parents split up, Dad pays Mum maintenance but it's never much according to her – although I have no idea how the money from the houses has actually been split up. I don't know any different and am grateful for what I have or what is given to me. Although I have some books, board games, Lego and toy cars, I don't have many toys; they are mostly secondhand. Around this time, 1974–75, Mum is a member of a Halifax Gingerbread Group for single parents who meet at each others' houses and take it in turns to hold a gingerbread evening. She makes friends and does things with them that also involve children, and she sometimes comes home with toys for me, which is always exciting.

Although we have little cash, Mum always makes sure I have the things I need and it's the same throughout my childhood. One day my friend George who lives across the fields gives me a bike. Mum can never afford to get me a bike because it's too expensive. I sometimes wonder whether Dad will think about buying me one, given his love of two-wheeled machines, but he's hardly ever around nowadays and I can only assume he's preoccupied with his own problems.

There's no point in my complaining about wanting a new bike, I'm never going to get one. George's old bike is definitely the next best thing. It is light green and beige and doesn't have a saddle, which makes it difficult to ride, but I'm not bothered. I think it's great. In any case the road we live in has a small dip so I stand on the pedals going down, get off at the bottom and push it back to the top.

For my sixth birthday, Mum gives me a red articulated truck. It is new, not secondhand, and I'm thrilled with it. I take it to school to show off to the other kids. It's great being the centre of attention for once and I feel so proud. Then one of the children takes a swipe at it, knocking it out of my hand. It crashes to the floor and breaks into pieces. All the kids go 'Ooooohhh!' and run off to avoid getting the blame.

I stand there, crying my eyes out, not because the toy is broken but because I know I won't get another new one. I hide it in my bag and don't tell Mum.

* * *

When she's not drinking she wants the best for me and she does this by being strict with me. She is anxious for me to do well in school and when we go on trips to other places in West Yorkshire and even to the seaside at Blackpool, she'll drag me around historical sites – maybe not kicking and screaming but sometimes a little reluctantly when I'd just like to have fun. Like her mother Sandra did to her, she pushes me hard, and keeps a close eye on me when it comes to schoolwork.

In stark contrast to how she is when she's drinking, when she is sober she won't tolerate bad behaviour. Once she makes her mind up on something, that is that. She always gets me to wash my hands before each meal and after I've finished eating I have to ask to leave the table. She believes in good manners and behaving myself in public, although this doesn't stop her doing embarrassing things herself.

One Saturday, when we're shopping in Halifax she buys me some fruitdrops and when I put one in my mouth I realize it's blackcurrant.

I pull a face and immediately take it out.

'Come on, David,' Mum is saying, 'we've got to get back home.'

'Can't we go to the toyshop and see the model railway, Mum?' I plead.

'No, I've told you once, we need to get home now.'

Mum has made up her mind and starts walking me towards the bus stop.

But I want to go and see the model railway in the toyshop and in a fit of pique I throw my fruitdrop on the ground.

We're in the middle of the town centre, milling with people, probably including children from my school. That doesn't worry Mum. She pulls down my trousers and smacks my backside in full view of anyone who is watching.

If Mum has decided on something and laid down the law, that's final. She won't allow any argument.

One evening, she makes kedgeree, a rice dish with fish. She is brilliant at baking but awful at cooking and as this is one of the few meals she can successfully cook, she often makes it. Although I can eat it, kedgeree is probably one of my least favourite meals, so I eat as much as I can stomach and leave the rest.

'Are you leaving that food?' Mum asks.

'Yes, I've had enough, Mum,' I reply.

'Right, well in that case, you will eat it for your breakfast.'

When she says something like that I know she means it. I'll have to eat it in the morning.

The meal has been bad enough the night before when it was warm and freshly cooked, but cold fish and rice for breakfast are disgusting. Yet the next morning, there it is, waiting for me. I struggle to get it down, doing every-thing in my power to stop myself throwing up.

This teaches me a lesson: not to upset Mum and to do exactly as I am told. From then on, I do this to the best of my ability, both through fear of reprisal and because, strangely enough, it makes me feel close to her. I rarely defy her and am always excited when she pays me a compliment.

* * *

The first Christmas after we move into the house on the far end of the block at Calder Bridge, Mum works very hard to turn it into something special: we decorate the house with crêpe paper and baubles on the tree, and there's a big bag of gifts on Christmas morning. The decorations are cheap but plentiful and we put them all over the house. Mum takes small items like chocolate bars and wraps them up in Christmas wrapping paper. It may not be quite the same thing as a real present but it helps make the bag look bigger and that's what matters to me.

I sneak down early on Christmas morning and start opening my presents. I feel a warm, glowing excitement and I want the day to go on forever. But I know this day will end and that sooner or later the Dark Mummy, the one who comes to me at night when she has been drink-ing, will return. And although I'm only six, I'm starting to realize that what she is asking me to do for her, and do to her, is very wrong.

My mother is drinking more than ever – I know that, because she is making me do things to her more often. It only seems to happen when she drinks and she never comes to me until she is badly drunk. That seems to happen quickly as soon as she starts drinking brandy.

It is always the same. She wants me to make her happy by rubbing her minnie. She never touches my willy or shows any interest in doing anything more than that. She takes my hand and places it on her minnie and rubs it.

But one thing is different now. Before, she needed to guide my hand and do it for me. But now that I'm older, I am learning to do it with less help from her. That seems to give her more pleasure and so it pleases me more.

I am totally unaware of the sexual and moral implications of what I am doing. I am just happy that Mum and I are doing something together that feels intimate. I am an affectionate and tactile child, loving to cuddle and be cuddled. And I feel that what has happened between us is a natural extension of that. But why she drinks and why she wants me to do these things for her is a closed book to me.

On the other hand, even as a six-year-old I know that Mum has been very lonely since she and Dad split up. Things have been difficult for her and yet she has driven Dad away through her difficult behaviour. I think she truly did love him and expected to spend the rest of her life with him. She is now solely responsible for bringing me up, and without any career or job to support her.

Mum can still be great company. She's in her late twenties and I sometimes see men looking at her and wanting to talk to her, but a few years later when I look back at this period it dawns on me that it must have taken an unusual man to accept her with all her problems, especially as at this stage she's had a six-year-old in tow.

From this time onwards, I begin to realize that the men closest to Mum are much older than her. They are the only ones who seem to be able to cope with how she is when she drinks. And around this time, something terrible happens as a result of her drinking which I'll remember for the rest of my life.

* * *

Mum has a friend called Charlie who lives in a small terraced house in a village called Mystendyke, not too far from where we live. Charlie has a beard and is tall and thin. To me, he seems very old but he's probably only in his sixties – certainly a lot older than Mum – and I'm not sure of the nature of their relationship. He's good company and I enjoy going there as he is always nice to me, telling me stories and jokes.

One night when we're there at his house, Mum gets steaming drunk and their conversation becomes really heated. Even though I'm only six, I have already seen this many times before and I know what's coming. They begin arguing and as each minute goes by, I can sense that it's about to get completely out of control.

Mum is now beside herself with rage. When drunk, she has no idea at all what's going on or any control whatsoever over her actions. Anything can happen and it often does.

She doesn't care about me either when she's like this. She's not a distant, unfeeling mother when she is sober, but on this night I can sense that I am surplus to requirements. Then something happens that changes all that. Somehow, in the course of the argument, she gets locked outside the house with me on the inside.

She is shouting bad words, banging on the window. I am completely bewildered by what is going on and just sit there crying. Of course, Mum hasn't tried to explain it to me and all I want is for her to be back inside the house.

'Charlie,' I'm crying, 'please let my mummy in!'

'No,' he shouts, 'she's not coming back in.'

By now she's at boiling point.

'*Let me in, you old bastard!*' she screams at Charlie through the glass.

'Not a chance!' he shouts back at her from inside.

She bangs harder until there is a sudden almighty crash as her fist goes through the window. Glass shatters all over the floor and my mother's head appears at the hole, her hand covered in blood where the glass has sliced it, blood dripping on the window ledge.

When, years later, I see Jack Nicholson's manic portrayal of the disintegrating writer Jack Torrence in Stanley Kubrick's film of Stephen King's horror novel *The Shining*, I can't help being struck by the similarity of the scene where Nicholson takes an axe to a wooden door, finally breaks through, pokes his heads through the shattered door and jeers at his terrified wife, '*Here's Johnny!*'

But, for me, at the age of six, the reality of seeing my demented mother's blooded fist breaking through the glass to be followed by her head is far more terrifying than any movie and it's a vision that will haunt me for the rest of my life.

She points and shouts abuse at Charlie at the top of her voice, telling him to let her in.

When he refuses, she turns on me.

'Open the door, David, *now!*' she screams.

I can see the obvious desperation of the situation even if I don't understand it, and I badly want to help her. I run to the door, trying to reach the latch, but can't quite make it.

'Come on, David,' she is shouting at the other side of the door. 'Come on!'

On the third attempt I succeed and release the latch. As Mum has been leaning on the door, and I have no time to move out of the way, it immediately swings open, bringing her full weight crashing down on me, knocking me to the floor. Completely oblivious to this, she leaves me there and, staggering along, pushes herself from one piece of furniture to the next, her hand dripping blood on the carpet, screaming at Charlie.

'You fucking bastard. Why wouldn't you let me in?'

Without giving him a chance to reply, she lunges at him, raining punches down on him again and again. They are inaccurate but he is an old man and he just sits in his chair, hardly able to defend himself. All he can do is curl up, trying to push away her flailing arms.

He is too old to retaliate.

She is too drunk to be reasoned with.

I am too frightened to speak.

All I have been trying to do is help her, but it feels as though in the process I have made things worse; and now Charlie is getting hurt too.

What is most shocking to me is the sudden unpredictability and volatility of my mother in this situation. For all I know she might well have killed herself, and Charlie, and even me in her drunken rage.

I'm so upset that I still can't speak for the rest of the night and even the next day I find myself keeping my distance from her, at least in my mind. I am looking at my mother differently now and what I see has changed something in me.

It may only be a small loss of innocence and trust, but from that night onwards I can never turn back the clock. I cannot make things better, or find my way back again to the mother I so long for her to be.

From that night onwards, my Dark Mummy is never far away.

* * *

Life with Mum is a rollercoaster. It doesn't help that by the time I am six Dad has met someone new and within a year has gone to live with her in Manchester many miles away from where we live in Yorkshire. Her name is Maureen and she lives there with her two sons, Harry and Alex, who I discover are two and four years older than me.

When I come downstairs one morning in the summer holidays of 1974 I find Mum crying. She's sitting at the kitchen table filling out a large, official-looking form in her careful, almost schoolgirl handwriting.

'What's the matter, Mum, why are you crying?'

'Nothing, David, just eat your breakfast.'

'What's that you're writing?'

'OK, if you want to know, I'm applying for legal aid. That's the only way I'm going to be able to afford to pay for solicitors.'

'Why do you Ford Slisters?'

'Never you mind, David, you'll understand one day.'

It takes me a while to work out that Mum and Dad are now no longer married legally and by this time it's 1975 and Mum tells me Dad has now married Maureen in Manchester. I can't understand why he hasn't invited Mum and me to the wedding. After all, we're still his family. Why wouldn't he want us there?

Maureen hasn't been involved in my parents' separation but this doesn't stop Mum hating her with a passion. She has managed to get a photo of her and has written 'Bitch' on the back.

I don't dislike my new stepmother. After all, I don't know her. I haven't even met her and nor has Mum as far as I know, but I'm intrigued as to why Mum hates her so much.

* * *

One day Mum and I are walking near our house when we see Rastus, our beloved orange and brown five-year-old collie, on the opposite side of the road at the top of the hill, some 50 yards away. Mum calls to him and he comes running down the hill towards us. We watch him all the way and as he gets to the road he doesn't stop. Before we know it he's been hit by a passing car just five yards in front of us.

There's a terrible screech of brakes and the next second the car stops twenty yards or so further up the road. But it's too late – Rastus has been killed instantly.

I can't quite grasp what's happened. It's the first time I've been brought face to face with death and after the shock I'm inconsolable. There's nothing we could have done to stop it but in my mind I keep re-running the incident like a video, trying to press Pause before Rastus reaches the road.

I cry for days.

Mum cries too as she loves her pets, especially Rastus. But although she's very sad, her response is actually quite calm and dignified. I don't know why, but I'm surprised as I expected her to be hysterical, like she is when she's drinking. It now occurs to me just how carefully she can keep her emotions under control when she's sober.

* * *

Dad returns to Halifax once a month and takes me to see his mother, my grandmother. They never talk at all about his father – my grandfather – and I often wonder about him. It seems that Dad has been brought up mainly by his mother and when he talks about his upbringing to me he described it with affection.

Grandma brushes my hair, which I like, and lavishes attention on me, which feels wonderful to me. It is unconditional and different from that of my mother. Although Mum's attention is certainly not conditional when she is sober, when drunk the only attention I get is when she wants me to touch her. She will decide how and when to show me affection – and nothing I do makes any difference. I may not fully understand this, but I sense it. Grandma, on the other hand, does that thing that grandparents do: she's highly attentive for a short period of time.

But Grandma has a strange side to her personality. She lives on her own – a quiet, eccentric, affectionate woman, with unusual views. She isn't very tall, walks with a slight stoop, and wears her long grey hair in a bun. Her house is like a junk shop, crammed with books, furniture and weird, exotic bric-a-brac, such as a carved wooden statue of three monkeys with their paws covering their eyes, mouth and ears.

'That means, see no evil, speak no evil, and hear no evil,' she says.

She'll talk about subjects I've never heard anything about in a fascinating way and I hang on to her every word. She knows a huge amount, does Gran, and I'm amazed and intrigued. I often wonder what it was like for Dad having her as a mother, with just the two of them living in the same house and how it must have affected him. I also wonder what he thinks about the things she tells me, but he just sits there in an armchair among the potted palms and peacock feathers while Gran talks to me; he's looking slightly bored and bemused, like he's heard it all before, and just lets her get on with it.

But, despite her crazy ideas, I love Grandma, which means that Dad doesn't have to work too hard to entertain me.

Nowadays it sometimes feels like Dad is simply going through the motions of being a father. I look up to him and desperately want him to be more involved. But he seems to have moved away emotionally as well as physically, never to return. He has chosen to be a distant parent and not get involved in my daily life. I can't work out whether it's because he doesn't care and can't be bothered, or because he simply doesn't have it in him.

* * *

It's really up to Mum to provide me with whatever it takes for me to have a happy and complete life and she can't do it either. Life with her seems to rock violently from one extreme to another.

But one thing she can do very well is make new friends. One of them lives just around the corner from the school in Calder Bridge. Mum's new friend has a daughter the same age as me called Katie. She is very pretty with a nice smile, long brown hair and she wears glasses. I often play with her and as I'm always keen to please, I'm happy doing anything Katie wants to do.

One evening at Katie's house, I am alone with her and decide to do what I do with Mum: I put my hand up her skirt and into her knickers. Her minnie feels different. It is smaller and there are no hairs. I start rubbing her in the same way as I do for Mum but Katie doesn't respond at all. This puzzles me as Mum always does, especially as I work hard to do it well.

After a short while she pushes my hand away and we play at something else. I don't mind because I don't think there's anything wrong with what we have done. It's just a game and we simply play another one that she likes.

* * *

By the time I'm seven, I know that Mum is drinking regularly. It isn't happening all the time – certainly not every day – and a lot remains hidden from me. I don't see her starting to drink. I only see the results when she has drunk a whole bottle. She is never just slightly drunk or tipsy: she is either sober or completely smashed.

In a rare moment of confession much later on in her life, she tells me that her main problem is that when she's opened a bottle of brandy she can't stop drinking it until it's empty.

Once drunk, she completely loses control, not just of her emotions but also her body.

And something else happens when she drinks in the evening. I remember the first time it happens …

* * *

Mum usually makes me tea when I come home from school but one day this doesn't happen. She lets me into the house but then goes off upstairs.

It feels like she's been gone a long, long time and she still hasn't come down and I'm getting very hungry.

'Mum, are you there? Where's my tea, Mum?' I finally call out.

'Be right down, David,' she replies after a minute.

More minutes go by and she still hasn't come down.

Then she does.

She's half undressed, and although she's trying to walk normally she's not quite steady on her feet as she comes into the living room where I'm sitting.

The clock on the mantelpiece says ten past seven and it's past my bedtime but Mum doesn't seem to notice.

'David!' she calls out as she sees me.

She staggers towards me and reaches down to hug me.

'David, give your mother a cuddle.'

Her words are slurred and I can smell the brandy on her breath as her face closes in towards mine.

'Can't we have tea, Mum? I'm hungry.'

'Yes, let's have tea, I'll make tea,' she says and staggers off into the kitchen.

I follow her, and I'm now feeling frightened but I'm not quite sure why. It's never happened before that she's forgotten to make me tea because she's been drinking.

Now she's trying to open a tin of baked beans and she's getting angry because the tin opener won't work.

She slams the tin down on the kitchen table and starts looking for a saucepan in the bottom cupboard but as she bends down she falls over.

'David, come here and give me a kiss,' she says angrily, forgetting that she's been trying to find the pan.

'Oh Mum, can't we just have tea?'

'David, do what your mother tells you!' she shouts.

I know better than to disobey her.

I join her on the floor and she pulls me towards her.

'Give me a kiss, David.'

I do what she says and instantly I can smell and taste the brandy on her mouth. I feel a little sick and finally pull away.

'Mummy, I'm tired. Can't we have tea now?'

'Yes, let's have tea,' she groans and tries to get up but collapses again on the kitchen floor ...

Mum never gets to make me tea this evening and that's the first time this has happened. She seems to have forgotten completely about my tea and even about me.

In the end I make myself a jam sandwich and put myself to bed but I stay awake for a long time, waiting to hear her come upstairs.

After what seems like another hour or more I hear her staggering to her bedroom and slamming her door shut.

Only then do I dare allow myself to go to sleep.

* * *

For me the first seven years of my life in Calder Bridge are a stark mixture of lightness and dark – I think of my earliest memories of playing as a child in a wonderful, exciting setting, the happy times playing in the woods and fields or in the scrapyard down the lane and I remember that one happy Christmas. But I also remember the sexual contact with my mother – the alcohol, mood swings, violence, blood, swearing and pain. Calder Bridge has created good memories and bad for me, but mainly I am haunted by the bad ones.

We are soon to move away from there, but the problems won't be resolved in our new home. Instead of life getting better, it is about to get much worse ...

3

A Man Called Reg

One day, when I'm seven, Mum takes me to see someone.
Reginald Arthur Brownstone is old, fat and bald, with a
huge ginger beard. Mum tells me she does some cleaning
for him. I have no idea why we're there, apart from allowing her to introduce me to one of her friends. It's a sunny
day and the house seems very impressive to me – detached
and in a beautiful setting, halfway up a valley.

Reg left school at the age of twelve because he was
needed on his father's farm. When I am introduced to him
he's still working in a textile factory but he only does so
for a few months longer after 53 years of work. He seems
a jovial man with a keen sense of humour. He certainly
makes Mum laugh and that hasn't been happening
enough.

Back home, Mum asks me what I think of Reg. I say he
seems OK. She's pleased with that and I feel good inside
too. I sense there is some kind of connection between them
and he seems like a nice, kind man.

By April 1975 we have moved out of our house in
Calder Bridge to live with him at his house in Ludden
Vale, near the village of Bradling. When we move in he is

already 65, while Mum is 30. But the age difference does-n't matter to me and moving in is great news. He is going to be the missing father figure in my life and make Mum happy. We have a new home and are destined to have a wonderful future together.

But unfortunately, Reg isn't all that he appears to be.

* * *

Because we have moved, I start at a new school, Bradling Primary. I like it immediately and it doesn't seem to have the problems of the old one. It is light and airy with large rooms and friendly teachers. There are lots of kids around where we live too. Even though our new house is rural, with only twelve houses in the immediate vicinity, there are eight kids aged within two years of each other and we start hanging around together.

Our house is just a couple of fields from a council estate where many kids from the school live. The estate is very nice and the house are well-maintained. But although the houses look great, going to the estate simply highlights how special our house is and how lucky we are to be living there.

Our new home is idyllic from the outside – a cluster of three early Victorian one-up–one-down cottages knocked into one, with lots of character – built on the side of a valley. The downstairs rooms from the three cottages form a group of three, the middle one (which we call the middle room) being the dining room. The house is detached and surrounded by fields and woodland, with a large garden full of fruit, vegetables, flowers and shrubs. The views from the front and back are breathtaking, showing the whole of the valley in one fell swoop. Inside, the house badly needed renovating. Reg has lived there a long time alone and hasn't bothered to do anything to the property in ages. But Mum is on the case and is going to get things done.

Living at Ludden Vale seems just as good as Calder Bridge but without all the bad memories, initially at any rate. This is a time to renew and start afresh. We are living as a family and in a beautiful family home.

Mum has been taking typing lessons at night school and is soon doing secretarial work as a full-time job. Although she isn't on a high wage, her money management is sensational. We go on holiday every year, have a nearly new car every three to five years and she manages to find the cash to get lots of work done on the house. We always have pets to look after too as both Reg and Mum are animal lovers. She smokes heavily and is still drinking. How she manages to do all this on the money coming into the house is a miracle. It helps that Reg owns the house outright: she doesn't need to borrow money or pay a mortgage.

Looking back on this all as an adult, I still find it astonishing that even with no mortgage she never fell into debt or borrowed any money, as far as I was aware, considering the double whammy of low household income and her drinking which must have drained her purse.

* * *

When we move into the house, to my relief, Mum's visits to my bedroom – the Special Time which I have now come to dread – suddenly come to a stop. As a seven-year-old I understand as little about why they stop as I understand why they started in the first place, but I think it's because now that Mum is sharing a bedroom with Reg she no longer needs me in the same way as before.

In any case, in the last few months of living at Calder Bridge, things have begun to change. I am now much more aware of what is right and wrong and have been feeling uncomfortable about what she makes me do when she's been drinking. I know we shouldn't be doing it and I have already begun trying to resist her. But until now I have always ended up doing as I was told, especially as she is so forceful and aggressive when she is drunk.

I think she is also drinking less as she is happier and more settled with Reg than she has been in a long time. I know that she always drinks more when she is feeling stressed or unhappy. So her demands for me to play with her seem to have ended, I have a new 'father' and Mum is drinking less. It feels like a brand new start and the house move seems to resolve the issues of my early life. We have security, stability, a home life and a family unit.

That's how it seems, at least.

* * *

In the first few months of living with Reg, Mum seems much happier. She loves gardening and sets about making the most of it. I think the garden looks a big mess and certainly isn't going to win any awards, but Mum grows rhubarb, gooseberries, redcurrants, blackcurrants, potatoes, cauliflowers and peas in the summer, tomatoes in the greenhouse, lots of flowers, particularly sweet peas, shrubs, plants and her own holly with proper red berries for the house at Christmas.

There's a small lawn and the whole garden is dry-stone walled so that passers-by can't look inside, which makes it nice and private. To me at the age of seven it is fantastic. However, as a garden it is drastically in need of remedial work and Mum does that over time as she loves gardening. As well as picking fruit in the garden, she spends many hours on a summer's evening and weekend picking wild blueberries and blackberries in the surrounding country-side and in summer she goes to Halifax market at teatime on a Saturday and bulk-buys strawberries that would otherwise be thrown away. The traders have to sell them cheap because, although they're fit to eat, they wouldn't last until Monday to resell.

She loves growing and picking fruit and making jams and jellies. She makes at least a hundred jars every year and we have every type of jam imaginable. She also heats fruit and puts it into Kilner jars which can later be used for making pies. She bakes every weekend and is very good at it. The biscuit tins are always full of fruit scones, parkin, flapjack, buns of all kinds, biscuits and fruit pies. Jam and baked foods are a staple part of our diet. Whenever I'm hungry, Mum tells me to 'go and get some jam and bread', which is a real treat.

Perhaps not surprisingly, I've started to develop a sweet tooth.

* * *

Not only is home life good but we now have an extended family. Reg's daughter Pauline lives only 200 yards up the road with her husband and their children. She is a dour, bespectacled woman who rarely smiles and wears her hair piled on top of her head. To begin with I'm a little wary of her, but she and her family welcome us into their family too.

Reg's brother Bert comes to visit him two or three times a year. Bert never knocks on the door and never comes into the house. He sits outside the house in his van, waiting for Reg to come out and talk to him. He's a man of even fewer words than Reg, distant and curt in his speech to the point where I've wondered why he even bothers to drive all the way over to see his brother.

'OK, Bert?' says Reg.

'Oh ay,' Bert will reply.

'I'm not bad myself.'

'Mmm.'

'Looks like rain.'

'Oh ay.'

Pauline's youngest son, Andrew, is a year older than me and is always coming down to the house. Andrew is fun to be around. He's a little taller than me and often seems to be laughing, but I sometimes sense a kind of malice in his laughter. He's mischievous, which makes things a little more intriguing. We have a chair in the living room that swivels around 360 degrees. We get told off if we get caught swivelling on it too much, but Andrew goes round at breakneck speed and hang the consequences.

It feels great to have someone I think of as family close by. My parents only have one sibling between them – my Uncle Jim, Mum's older brother. I know he has been married at least once and I have cousins somewhere but I've never met them. I have even discovered that one of my cousins was born on the same day as me, which fascinates me and I want to meet her. But despite the fact that my uncle is collecting children and cousins that I never see, Andrew is as good as family to me. He lives nearby and we play together.

We have an even stronger connection when it comes to 'naming' Reg. His grandfather is my new father and the whole family situation is sealed when we agree I will call Reg 'Grandad', just like Andrew and his brothers and sisters do.

Reg can be very kind in these first few months and when he's got time at the weekends he'll spend time with me while I ride around on an old bike.

'Easy on the brakes, lad,' he'll say. 'Gently does it and if you just want to slow down but not stop, open them up again the same way, gently.'

I do as Reg says and it makes a big difference. I become more confident on the bike, and I'm soon whizzing around Ludden Vale and Bradling.

I can't believe my luck and decide that Reg is the bee's knees.

But things can't last that well forever.

* * *

The first thing to bring my wonderful new life crashing down comes about when Mum and Reg decide to build another bedroom. Up until now I have been sleeping in the room next to Reg and Mum's room. My bedroom is a like a junk room with a camp bed in it. The room is bigger than my old bedroom at Calder Bridge but because it's so full of bits of broken furniture, gardening equipment, old clothes which I think must have belonged to Reg's old family, and other bric-a-brac, there's barely room to move, and the camp bed isn't too comfortable either, though I put up with it.

During the first summer at Ludden Vale, Reg and Terry, a builder friend, build a second storey on top of the kitchen on one end of the house to create a new bedroom for me. The room I've been sleeping in – which will now be the upstairs middle room – is to be turned into another living room, though in reality it will be Mum's room where she can spend time on her own, maybe to have a little space from Reg as for the last few years since Dad left she's been used to living on her own.

It's amazing to see it develop and all summer I help Reg and Terry as much as I can. They are both retired so they are over 65 and it's quite a task for them both. I sense this and do as much as I can to help them. My favourite task is to have my own measuring tape and fetch a stone of a specified height. Reg sends me off looking for what he needs and I run around until I find one.

I am dazzled and amazed by the building work. To me it seems almost magical that out of all this brick and stone and mortar we – Reg, Terry and I – have managed to conjure up a part of the house that looks to my eyes as if it has always been there. I'm very proud of it.

I'm also discovering how clever Mum is – she has a knack of making money stretch a long way and getting things done. She finds the money to get this extra bedroom built, to renovate the rest of the house, install a new fitted kitchen, and re-paper and re-carpet every room. She has fresh furniture put in too. This may not be new but it doesn't matter. She knows how to find good quality secondhand furniture at bargain prices, all on a secretary's wage and a retired man's state pension.

Working with Reg on the building and the praise he gives me has been wonderful. I feel that he wants me there, and that, for the first time in my life, there is a father–son bond between us that I've never had with my own father. But in reality, building a new bedroom means something very different: I am getting my own room.

This is to cause me more pain than anything else in my childhood although for the time being I am delighted at having my own space. But one of the barriers preventing my mother from gaining full access to me has been removed.

* * *

Another thing that has changed at Ludden Vale is that we have our first family holiday. From now on 'holiday' for me means staying in tents on campsites.

I hate camping, particularly as we don't have good quality gear when we first start. Camping is rough at the best of times but when the three of us are squashed into a small tent without decent protection and waterproofing it can be downright miserable if the weather turns against us. In the next few years we go all over the country camping, although on this first holiday camping trip with Reg we actually break this rule by staying for two nights in a hotel in Paignton, Devon. This feels so luxurious, especially as our house in Ludden Vale has still not been renovated. I love the sea air and it feels like a real adventure travelling so far.

I am used to going to the seaside as Mum has occasion-ally taken me to Blackpool, on England's north-west coast, to see the illuminations. But Devon is different. It feels wild and exotic.

Once on holiday we're determined to make the most of it. Family photos show us enjoying ourselves on the sands and paddling in the sea. This is really my first family holiday as I don't remember any with Mum and Dad in my years at Calder Bridge.

But one thing hasn't changed for Mum as a result of moving in with Reg. It isn't long before she starts drinking heavily again. Her need is too great and she must feel she can get away with it – after all, he is 66 and she is only 31. When I'm older it occurs to me that one of the reasons she was with someone so much older than her was that she was able to have her own way with Reg.

In the first year we live with Reg he never seems to drink much and then after that he stops drinking altogether. I don't know if this is so that he can help Mum when she's drinking and unable to look after herself or if he's just decided to stop of his own accord. In any case, he isn't the kind of man to spend time in a pub chatting with his mates so I don't think it's an issue for him or that he misses it. For whatever reason he doesn't drink like Mum, though, and I'm grateful for the fact.

On the second night at the hotel, however, Mum does get drunk and it marks a turning point in my life.

* * *

I have been in bed for some time when she comes into my hotel bedroom. She's plainly drunk as she staggers in, switches on the light and sits at the end of my bed.

'David,' she says, in a whisper.

I don't wake up.

'David!' she says more loudly.

I wake up with a start, wondering what's going on. I don't know what time it is but going by Mum's drinking pattern, it must be around 10 pm.

'What's happening, Mum?' I ask, blinking in the light and rubbing my eyes.

'Nothing, David,' she says. 'I just want to know if you love me.'

'Yes, Mum,' I say, just wanting to roll over and go back to sleep.

'Well, give me a kiss then.'

'Aw, Mum, do I have to?'

'Yes. Go on. Give me a kiss, on the lips.'

She is reeking of alcohol and as she leans her open mouth towards me I start to feel sick. She tries to kiss me with her open mouth and for a moment I get a sensation of her tongue on mine. It feels odd and furry and strange and I want to recoil from it, but I know that the most important thing I can do is to satisfy her so I give her the kiss she wants. All I want to do is go back to sleep and forget about it.

I wipe my lips clean and she doesn't even notice me doing so as she has climbed on to my bed and is pulling my hand towards her.

'Play with me, David, play with your mummy. Mummy wants you to play with her.'

She's making me rub her down there and she's starting to moan and as usual I do what she wants me to do.

At last I can tell that she's got what she needs. Without another word she gets off the bed and leaves my hotel bedroom, turning the light off as she goes.

* * *

What is so different about this incident from what went on at Calder Bridge before we moved to Ludden Vale is that there has been an interval where she has left me alone. In these few months I have changed. I now know for sure that what she wants from me is wrong and yet, now more than ever, I know that I must please her and satisfy her, because I'm frightened of consequences of not doing so far more than before.

As the days and weeks and months go on, so does Mum's drinking – as well as her growing control over Reg. It's obvious to me that he is so grateful to be with an attractive woman 35 years his junior that he is prepared to put up with anything. It never fails to amaze me how pliable Reg is in Mum's hands and how much she dominates him. To the vast majority of men it might be seen as unacceptable behaviour but Reg is quite prepared to put up with it just to be with my mother. He has retired from the mill and is effectively a househusband, looking after me when I come home from school and doing household chores – not easy for a man of his age.

Every evening Reg will open the garage for Mum. It's a short distance from the house up a steep lane. When she comes past the house going up the lane she beeps her horn; he then has to drop whatever he is doing and dash up to the garage. She turns the car round and he has to have the garage doors open by the time she is ready to drive in. Even though by now I am eight years old I can never work out why Reg has to run out and open the garage doors for her and why she doesn't do it herself. Once in the house, he has to make her a cup of tea and sit at the table with her while she relates the day's events. For

Mum, this inevitably means bitching about someone at work.

With family or friends, at the vets or other social areas Mum is happy to mix with others and will talk the hind legs off a donkey. But she seems to find it difficult at work. She often comes home and complains about the other girls in the office. I get the feeling she's on the outside looking in. I don't think she goes for a drink after work or joins her work colleagues in social events and I think she finds working with other people quite stressful.

At home, even small things can cause a major row. Reg is old and often seems to float around in a world of his own. One thing he regularly does is leave the door open. Mum will go ballistic, especially if he doesn't jump up to shut it immediately.

'Reg, you've left the door open.'

'OK, well you're stood there. Please shut it.'

'Why the hell should I shut the door for you? You left it open.'

'But, Carol, you're stood there. Just shut the door.'

'I'm not shutting the door for you. You're the one who left it open, as always.'

'But I'm sat down now. Please shut the door, Carol.'

By now, she is incandescent with rage. '*Reg!* Get up and shut this door *right now!*'

At this point, Reg has lost the will to live, let alone fight about the open door so he'll get up, glare darkly at Mum and slam the door shut.

She needs to be in control in every area of our lives – of Reg as much as of me – even when sober. She dictates when to go shopping, planning holidays, what to buy for the house, what to watch on television and even what time she and Reg go to bed. He just falls into line. Later in my life I realize that most men wouldn't have put up with it but Reg does and manages it well.

For me, there is the same pressure to do exactly what she says. Mostly, this means doing chores and keeping time. When playing out I often go to Andrew's and even venture as far as the estate. Mum isn't too bothered where I go as long as I am back on time. If I am close to returning even slightly late, I panic and get really stressed out. I would rather run until my lungs are on fire than be late home. If I am late, I never hear the last of it and she will restrict future playing out times.

In the house, dealing with Mum is about doing the jobs she asks of me. From an early age I have a daily cleaning job. Fridays, for example, means cleaning the cooker. I don't mind, except that she doesn't seem to do it at all, so it's never a simple wipe down but always requires hard scrubbing. She also makes me clean my shoes every day on newspaper on the kitchen floor and as I get older she shows me how to iron my clothes.

Later as a teenager I will have to iron all my own clothes and perform many domestic chores in the house. No doubt she is teaching me this so that I can do jobs in the house that she doesn't have to do. But it does help me to develop valuable skills and teaches me to be independent.

Despite her overbearing behaviour, Reg is happy to put up with it, and I am too young to complain or think any differently. Besides, in the beginning it creates something I have never experienced before: a proper family life. We are living as a family unit in a nice house.

But it can't last. Cracks are starting to appear. My first awareness of this is an odd intimation that Reg has quickly lost interest in being a father. Mum's drinking is starting to increase and her behaviour when drunk is just as erratic as at Calder Bridge. I am soon beginning to realize that although I thought I had left the bad memories behind, they have actually followed me to our new house and new, worse ones are about to be created.

Mum once told me that life had been difficult for her with Dad and I think that may have influenced her decision to come to me for physical affection. I have no recollection of them being affectionate with each other or Dad being affectionate to me. Most people have at least one good parent. I now have three bad ones: an absent father who shows me little love or affection, a mother whose demands for something more than affection are to rise again and inflict themselves upon me, and a stepfather whose behaviour towards me is about to change in a way I could never have expected.

I have no-one to turn to, no-one to confide in and help me through the dark times. I have to deal with all that is coming my way on my own. As a young boy this becomes a torture for me. It turns me into a lonely, disturbed, angry child, which in the months and years to come is to have serious long-term consequences for me and those around me.

4

Smashing the Dream

The first twelve months at Ludden Vale with Reg seem like a kind of paradise to me. Reg has provided us with a beautiful home and he and Mum seem to get on well. He is a practical man, having worked with his hands all his life, and is always doing something to make our home a nicer place. On one of his monthly visits Dad even says that he owes Reg a debt of gratitude for providing his son with a home. At the time he is absolutely right: we are able to experience life in a new, richer way, through the various seasons. And because of the beautiful location, our quality of life is as much to do with the landscape as the house.

Our first autumn and winter at the house are different from anything I have experienced previously. Bonfire night is the second best day of the year after Christmas. With all the woodland around our house, we go plotting for wood to make a bonfire in the garden. There is always an endless supply to create huge bonfires and all the neighbours join us for Bonfire Night. Mum goes wild, making food and loves being hostess, making traditional bonfire food like hot dogs, toffee, parkin and flapjack – an absolute feast. I find myself stuffing my face, as it is so much better than our usual plain diet. Mum has bought a big box of Standard fireworks and Reg puts on a cracking show. Because of the size of the garden, we can accommodate all the different fireworks – sparklers, rockets and standalone fireworks as well as Catherine wheels attached to the bird table. The garden is a blaze of colour and sound and it's a truly magical night.

Winter is always the best season at Ludden Vale. Living on the side of a valley, we have the perfect landscape for sledging. We have snow in the first year, and Reg's grandson Andrew and I spend hours getting soaked going up and down the hillsides. We can't afford a plastic sledge like some of the other kids but that doesn't matter because Reg has made us a sledge. In fact, I am very proud that we have a 'dad' or 'granddad' who cares enough to want to make us a sledge. It is concocted from old pieces of wood with plastic runners on the bottom. It works perfectly well and if it gets damaged at all, Reg will just fix it back up again.

Christmas Day is the best day of the year, especially as everyone makes a big effort and I feel like they've put me at the centre of the occasion. Mum not only doesn't drink excessively but she really pulls out all the stops when it comes to presents. She never spends a lot of money but she will take small gifts and wrap them up and make sure I have a sizeable pile. I soon work out that I'm not getting a lot of 'proper' gifts and that some are quite small but it's still a lot of fun to open them. Reg and Mum work hard all morning and in the afternoon we have a fabulous traditional Christmas meal. On two occasions Grandma comes for Christmas and just sits in a chair without moving all day.

Living in the house is wonderful, but no amount of holly or bonfire toffee can mask the real issues that are about to smash the dream.

* * *

The first major change I notice is in Reg. He seems to have lost interest in me and has become offhand and surly with me. It is as if he doesn't like me anymore and doesn't want me in his house. This isn't good, especially as I'm at an age where I'm still keen to learn about the world around me. I like to ask questions and Reg doesn't want to answer them. He's supposed to be looking after me when I come home from school as he has now retired and Mum is working full time, so when I come through the door he's the first person I see.

'Guess what we learned today, Grandad,' I say excitedly, taking my raincoat off and hanging it on a hook by the front porch.

Reg sighs wearily, but otherwise doesn't rely.

Undaunted, I carry on. 'We learned all about rainfall. Do you know where rain comes from, Grandad?'

He has already sat down by the fire and now has his face buried in the local evening paper, checking the race results.

'It comes from the sea and then the sun heats it all up and that's called evaporation and then it all turns into clouds and then when there's lots of clouds you get condensation *and then you get rain!*' I finish triumphantly, but Reg hasn't even bothered to look up, let alone reply.

The penny soon starts to drop: he's not interested in what I've learned at school. In fact he's not interested in anything I have to tell him. It soon becomes obvious that he just wants to do the bare minimum in his dealings with me. His sole interest is in Mum. I know that he and Mum have an odd, imperfect relationship but they certainly seem to love each other. I, on the other hand, am surplus to requirements as far as Reg is concerned. And soon after this I discover just how surplus to Reg's requirements I really am.

One day, I'm playing in the house after school and watching television. Out of the blue, Reg starts shouting at me, saying I have done something wrong. I have never experienced this before from him. He has never shouted at me. I have seen him shout at Mum in an argument but never at me. I'm still not sure what I've done but from this time onwards one thing that definitely winds him up is when he calls me and I don't come immediately – just like it makes Mum angry when he doesn't immediately do what he tells her.

I look at him in horror. I don't quite know what's going on but I do know this is really bad. Reg shouts at me again and starts coming towards me, eyes blazing, fists clenched. I jump up and run upstairs to my bedroom, shutting the door and putting my back against it, hoping in my childlike innocence that I can hold him back if he comes up the steps.

I can hear Reg, nearly 70 years old, fat and wheezing, climbing the steps. He stops at the top to regain his breath and balance, then slowly plods towards my room, pushes down the handle and tries opening the door with his arm. He can't do it as I am pushing with all my might on the other side. He leans against the door a second time but this time puts his shoulder and all his weight into it. My weight is no match for his and he sends me flying into the middle of the room, falling into a heap on the floor, as he crashes through the open door.

I look up into his eyes and can see that he's really mad. I have no idea what I've done to make him so angry but know I need to get away from him. I fling myself into the far corner of my bedroom, crouching down as low and far away from him as possible, instinctively curling up into a tight ball. I don't know why I am so scared. After all, he has never hit me before. I just assume he'll shout at me but I want to put myself into a protective position, just in case. He comes across the room and leans over, his eyes raging, and slowly inches towards me.

'Think you can get away from me, do you?' he puffs, still out of breath from climbing the steps.

'No,' I say, not daring to look at him for fear of making him even more angry.

'Well, you can't, so take that.' He raises his fist and swinging it fast, brings it crashing down on top of my arm near my shoulder.

I let out a cry. 'Stop, Grandad,' I plead, 'please stop.'

'I'm going to teach you a lesson,' he says.

I will hear these words many times again.

Reg then swings his left arm and punches me in the stomach. I move my arm to protect my stomach but then he punches me again on the arm. As he keeps on punching me I do my best to protect myself, but I can't do so every-where and he keeps punching me where I'm not covering myself. After ten or fifteen punches rain down, he stops and looks at me.

'Right, don't cause any more trouble or you'll get it again.'

It's as though whatever I've done to switch on his anger, it seems to be all but burnt out by the time he has finished cornering me and giving me a good hiding.

He wanders off downstairs. All the way down I can hear him trying to regain his breath.

From this time on when he beats me I come to wish he would stop breathing altogether and keel over. He always looks like he's about to have a heart attack or a stroke when he's hitting me and I sometimes think that that would be a suitable punishment for someone who picks on and hurts a young boy for almost no reason at all.

I stay in the bedroom, waiting for him to calm down, not daring to go downstairs until I feel at least a little confident that he won't hit me again.

In my mind, I'm trying to work out what is going on, trying to understand what has triggered his anger and the violence. And I want to wait until the pain has gone away. No-one has hit me like that before and I'm hurting really badly. My arms throb and my stomach hurts. I sit there in the corner of my bedroom, quietly sobbing to myself, nursing my bruised and painful body, rocking myself back and forth.

* * *

I am eight years old and I don't know what has triggered this assault. I have done nothing wrong. As a child, I have learned to be highly submissive with my mother and I'm the same with Reg. I am keen to please and often look to do something to make him happy, not make him mad. Besides, Mum has already given me the hard word, telling me I must behave when she isn't there as she is having to go out and work to earn money for the family. I under-stand this and don't want to rock the boat. I just assume I've been a naughty boy and deserve to be punished.

When I have time to think about what's happened I start to wonder if it's because of Reg's upbringing and background. He is a fat man but also big and strong, even for his age. He has done hard manual labour all his life, working in farming, joinery and mill work. He lost the sight of one of his eyes as a child after an accident with a bike pump and has even chopped one of his fingers off in a circular saw. His fists are huge and rock hard.

As a child he lost his mother at the age of twelve and was up by his father on a working farm. He has already told me how he had to work very long hours as a boy and has spoken about fights he used to get into as a young lad and even though he was quite a fanciful storyteller, it's obvious he has learned to handle himself. He's come from the school of hard knocks and I'm a very soft boy. Maybe he thinks I need toughening up. But one thing's for sure. It can't have been because I am habitually naughty. Like all kids, I do something naughty occasionally but I'm never malicious or nasty and I'm not a naturally feisty or argumentative child. My school reports indicate that I'm well behaved at school, never rude or cheeky.

Maybe I blame myself for being too weak and submissive; maybe deep down I believe that I somehow allowed Reg to beat me up, almost invited him to, just as I wonder if it's possible that in some way I have allowed what goes on between Mum and me to happen. Maybe my lack of self-esteem has something to do with my Special Time with Mum: I want to please her but I also fear displeasing her.

In the regular beatings he gives me from now on Reg never hits me in the face. I presume this is so that Mum won't find out. Considering she might see me with no clothes on at some stage, I hardly think this is a guaranteed way of keeping my beatings hidden, but that isn't the point. Reg can't control himself when his inner rage spills over. When he feels the need, nothing less than punching the hell out of me will do. The look says it all as his eyes reveal the disgust, malice and venom he feels towards me. Whatever I have done to make him feel like that isn't going to go away by his counting to ten.

But even he knows that letting Mum see me with a smashed-up face will be too much.

* * *

The beatings start slowly and gather pace. He never does it on a daily basis but they are regular and painful. He will never hold back from hitting me and it leaves me scared to be alone in the house with him. Despite all my previous issues with Mum, she never beat me and Reg never does it when she is there. So I often sit in my bedroom after school, watching for her coming up the road in the car and running downstairs to meet her. This reassures me that a beating isn't going to happen for this day at least.

But even since he has started beating me, Reg can still be nice when he wants to be and if the mood takes him, he is great to be around. The problem is I can never second guess what mood he's going to be in when I get in from school. I pray it is the nice man who will be making my tea when I walk through the door. My mother's split personality has already made life very difficult for me – and now Reg is doing exactly the same. It's not knowing what mood he's going to be in that causes me such anxiety and fear. The constant listening and trying to gauge what Reg is thinking is almost impossible for me at my age.

I will never forget the thumping of my heart as I walk through the door every night, wondering what might be coming my way.

Mum has settled down in her relationship with Reg and is being a pretty good mother. She can be loving and affectionate, and for me as a child who needs that, it is great when we're close, especially as she isn't asking me to do things to her any more. On the other hand, I'm always on the lookout for her drinking, because I know what that means – a massive, immediate change in her behaviour.

In spite of everything that's happened between us, she tries to be a responsible parent, making sure I have everything I need. She encourages me to join the Cubs in the next village and I go there every Friday night. I love it so much I join the Scouts at the age of eleven. I go away on weekend trips, campfires, orienteering and staying up all night. Whereas camping as a family feels like a cut-price holiday for poor people, combined with having nothing to do when we get there, scout camping is the opposite. It's exciting being with a bunch of lads staying up until the middle of the night with games and activities all day.

My school reports are scrutinized down to the last detail; if anything is slightly unsatisfactory she's onto the school immediately to put it right. I find this a bit of a mixed blessing. It's good that she cares, but I'm always anxious about her seeing my reports, and sometimes I find her interventions on my behalf – the way she makes a fuss at school – over the top and embarrassing. But I put up with it, because I've got no choice, and I know she has my best interests at heart.

At school one week we're doing history and the teacher tells us all about people called dictators. There was Adolf

Hitler who was the leader of the Nazis who Britain fought in the last war under Winston Churchill. And there's Joseph Stalin who was a ruthless dictator in the Soviet Union though he wasn't quite as bad as Hitler. Then there was Mussolini, who my teacher calls a tinpot dictator. They want to be big and powerful like the really bad dictators but they don't quite make it.

And there are others, says my teacher, who are good dictators. She calls them benevolent dictators because although they're very strict they want to make life better for people. One of these, she says, is a Cuban leader called Fidel Castro and she shows us a picture of him. I decide that Mum's must be a bit like a benevolent dictator. I wonder if Fidel Castro also gets drunk at night.

Mum's like a benevolent dictator over my reading. She's an avid reader herself and she takes me down to the local library every week, telling me I have to choose a book. She gives me complete freedom to choose any book I want, but I've got to choose it and I've got to read it. My favourite is Billy Bunter.

Mum's a benevolent dictator about my health. It seems to nag at her. She'll stand over me to make sure I clean my teeth properly every day and I never miss an appointment at the dentist or the doctor. And every Saturday we go to Halifax town centre. Reg never joins us, which makes it better too.

We go first to the Good As New shop on Clare Road. Mum always gets me secondhand clothes, a simple, effective way to ensure I always have plenty of clothes. As long as they're in decent condition, that's fine by her. She is also an incredible knitter and on evenings and weekends knits me many jumpers to wear. The only things she always buys brand new are shoes. During this period – the mid-1970s – plastic shoes are popular as a more cost-effective option, but Mum makes sure I have leather shoes because they mould to the shape of my feet properly even though they cost more money.

After a swim in Halifax pool we go to the library and then it's time for lunch at a café. I spend ages pondering over the menu, deciding what to have. There are lots of meals I never have at home or at school. I always have bread with margarine: at home we only have butter and I much prefer the taste of margarine even though it's considered the poorer option. Finally we go to Halifax indoor market to buy fresh meat, fruit and vegetables. I love the hustle and bustle of market traders with their patter and special offers.

Those days are special and I feel like a son should towards his mother, like she's the best mother in the world. But as much as she has the ability to give, she can also take away without a moment's hesitation or warning. I know this from our time at Calder Bridge as I can still vividly remember the Special Time and the drunkenness. Mum's behaviour can turn in an instant and the contrast can be as different as night and day. But I also know that alcohol is the trigger for all the bad things that happen, and she hasn't been drinking much recently as far as I am aware.

But that is all about to change.

***

Even though I have often feared it, I haven't really appreciated until now that the dark side of Mum's personality is never far from the surface and it's certainly too much to hope that it has gone away for good.

I don't know what has triggered her drinking again but suddenly it's back with a vengeance. She has never developed the ability to control her alcoholism and it is now time for it to reappear. Once it does, it's back for good: for the rest of her life she will never again get it under control. By now she has developed a definite drinking pattern and I know exactly what she does.

When I arrive home from school these days, she has very occasionally already started drinking – even if only in small amounts – and I have learnt to tell the signs. She will be slightly unsteady on her feet, her speech fractionally slurred, but only in a way that I would notice – I have no idea whether Reg also notices as he never speaks to me about this or anything else. More often than not, though, she is still quite sober and remains so until after supper.

Then she goes upstairs.

She always drinks brandy and takes the full bottle up to her bedroom to which she disappears every fifteen minutes or so. She drinks heavily and quickly, and then comes back downstairs.

From the first visit to her room, there is a marked difference in her body and voice. She immediately starts staggering about and slurring her words. Within an hour of having her first sip she is reeling all over the place, completely smashed.

'*Get out of my way, you fucking bastard!*' she screams at Reg as she lurches around the living room.

Reg tries to calm her down but to no avail. She is uncontrollable; he is an old man. It doesn't help that she is also very agitated. Once drunk, she can't stay still, constantly wandering around the house. She's up and down the stairs, turning the television on and off and shouting at the top of her voice.

By now she's usually half dressed, just wearing something covering the top half of her body. This in itself is distressing for me and it isn't good for her either as she has no protection for her legs. We have stone steps in the house and she always seems to have bruises on her legs from falling down the steps at least once every evening when she gets drunk. This will be the pattern until we go to bed. Once in bed, she rarely rouses me. She'll eventually get tired of wandering around then go to bed herself. On at least one occasion, though, this isn't the case.

* * *

I get up at what feels like the middle of the night but in reality is probably about midnight. I go to the toilet and as I came out I notice the lights and television are on downstairs so I wander down to investigate. I look in the front room first where the television is, but there's no-one there. I switch it off, and look in the middle room but that's empty too, apart from the dogs. We always have two dogs while I'm at home. The dogs are a Labrador/Collie cross and a Westie. I love the dogs, especially as it's mainly my job to walk them. I fuss over them for a little and then go into the kitchen. What I see there horrifies and alarms me.

Mum is lying on the floor in the foetal position. She is absolutely still and appears to be dead. She is half naked, which is usual when she's been drinking, and is wearing nothing but her knitted jumper. She is surrounded by what looks like cooking oil that she has probably spilt trying to cook something on the cooker. *The cooking oil is full of live and dead matches that she must have been using to try and light the gas to cook the food.*

I bend down and try to wake her up.

'Mum,' I whisper in her ear, 'Mummy, wake up.'

She murmurs something.

I speak to her again but a little louder. 'Mummy, it's me, David. Please wake up.'

While speaking, I shake her body and pull on her shoulder. As I do so, she starts to regain consciousness and rolls over quickly towards me. She instinctively raises her arm and, with the momentum of her body, inadvertently punches me straight in the mouth.

I am shocked and shaken. Although I'm used to getting a beating from Reg, I'm not used to being hit by Mum, and not used to being hit in the face at all. I know she hasn't done it on purpose but even so, it's still a nasty surprise. I back away to let her get up.

Mum opens her bleary eyes and glances around, unable to focus properly. She looks at me and then tries pushing herself off the slippery floor to stand up. She eventually manages to drag herself up by the kitchen sink and then holds onto one of the worktops for support.

'Are you alright, Mummy?' I ask.

She makes no acknowledgement at all. She has a slow look around the kitchen. She seems to see me but then looks straight through me and staggers off through the house, using the walls and furniture to keep her from falling, eventually finding her way to her bedroom.

Throughout this terrible ordeal, she never says a word to me or checks to see if I have got to bed OK.

I leave the kitchen as it is and go to bed myself.

* * *

This incredibly serious situation and lucky escape for the whole family is an example of just how out of control Mum is when drunk. She could have turned the gas on and left it going, potentially blowing the whole house up and the three of us with it. The matches could have ignited the gas at any moment or even set her on fire. The hot oil she was using to fry some food could have badly injured her or caused a fire itself.

My mother is an intelligent woman. She must have understood how bad things are, especially when coming down in the morning to the devastation of the night before. She must have woken up with an empty brandy bottle next to her bed and seen the volume of alcohol she had consumed. But she has no ability whatsoever to limit her drinking or stop it at all. Her addictive personality means that she has to drink and continue drinking until she can't drink any more.

Despite her heavy drinking, there are never any half-empty brandy bottles around the house. What she does is to buy a single bottle at a time and drink it all in one evening. This will take only about an hour and she never has it with any mixers. She drinks the whole bottle neat and then quietly disposes of the bottle. Not for Mum a big bag of empty bottles and cans to take to the tip as a stark reminder of her drinking habit. This way she is able to deceive herself into thinking that she isn't like other people with a drinking problem. She never thinks she is as bad as other people. This self-delusion means that she doesn't seem to consider the effect her drinking has on Reg and me. We do not discuss in the morning what has happened the night before.

I'm just glad she's safe and in any case I'm too young to bring up the issue. Besides, when Mum is sober she's a good mother and it's easy for me to assume that she must understand what she is doing. And, of course, I don't know any different. I go to other kids' houses but I don't talk about her drinking. I assume it is normal and that every parent does it, even though it causes me a lot of stress.

Most children of my age look to their parents for guidance and help as they go through life. For me, it's the other way round. I am already, as an eight-year-old, spending many nights staying up, sometimes into the early hours, making sure she gets to bed. Mum spends a lot of the evening wandering around the house, so I stay awake, listening to make sure that she will eventually go to sleep which she always does. Reg doesn't help her – he leaves her to it.

In some ways it is fulfilling because I'm helping Mum who I love, but it isn't a job for a child to have to perform. Yet, throughout this period, I am incredibly relieved that the Special Time has stopped. That has been a horrible and difficult period for me, but it has not been a part of my life for some time. It is now difficult and psychologically stressful for me, but listening out for Mum doesn't put me at such risk of physical danger or having to obey her other demands when she used to ask me to do things to her.

All that is in the past – or so I think. But I'm too young to know that things can keep changing, or that they can turn back on themselves so that the past can reappear in a new, shocking way.

5

Easy Access

Why Dad hasn't invited me to his wedding when he married Maureen is one of many unanswered questions I've wanted to ask him. While living in Manchester he drives over to Halifax to see me one Sunday in every month.

I'm always excited when I know he's turning up. Dad takes me to see Grandma and she then takes over the reins to entertain me for the day. He is happy for her to feed and mollycoddle me while he sits looking on.

On this particular Sunday morning I'm feeling more bruised than usual from the beating Reg gave me yesterday when Mum was out shopping and visiting a friend. As always it came without warning. I was sitting on the floor in the living room watching television and when Reg said something to me I couldn't have heard what he said – I don't even know if I responded or not, but it was obviously not quick enough, because he came at me before I had a chance to get to my feet and run upstairs.

'I'll teach you to ignore me when I'm talking to you!'

Before I could even speak or cry out in protest he began smashing his fist into my arms, stomach and thighs. I was doubled up on the floor in pain, but he still kept coming at me for minutes that seemed like hours. Finally, though, he seemed to run out of steam and left me there, whimpering on the rug.

When Mum came home an hour later I said nothing, and although she must have seen I was upset, she said nothing either.

This morning there are nasty purple bruises at the top of my legs and arms, but the clothes I'm wearing are covering them up, just like the blanket of silence that muffles up what's really going on between the three of us.

Dad comes as usual but this time he drives me all the way to Manchester. I'm still smarting from the bruises on the journey and wish I could say something to Dad about what's been happening, but I don't know how to. Dad's just too distant with me on the drive and talks as usual about cars, bikes and sport. He doesn't really ask me how I am, or not in a way that would let me tell him what I've been going through. He just doesn't seem interested enough. So I end up as usual saying nothing, just as I say nothing to Mum about what she and Reg are both doing to me.

I forget about all this though when we arrive in Manchester and at last I get to meet Maureen for the first time. She's wonderful and I start thinking of her as my stepmother. She's affectionate and attentive and looks after me really well. She doesn't seem to have Mum's split personality: there's no alcohol, no arguments, shouting or beatings – and certainly no demands for me to play with her at night.

Life with Dad and Maureen in their comfortable house in the suburbs of Manchester is very different from life at Ludden Vale and I begin to realize that the way Mum, Reg and I live isn't the norm for all families as I had previously assumed. Being with him in Manchester I can get more of his attention and enjoy the good things about Dad.

He still has his cars and bikes in his garage and shows me them all. He's patient and quiet as usual, the exact opposite of Mum and Reg. He has always been a calming influence in my life, never shouting or being abusive, and always answers any questions I have, no matter how stupid they are.

We visit Dad's workplace. I'm very impressed by this because he has a huge desk in his office. I know he's one of the best at what he does in the UK at this time and is in demand in other parts of the world too for his abilities and expertise. He started off as a draughtsman and is now an expert in galvanizing, a way of coating steel to make it rust resistant. I also know that he has some kind of managerial job.

I'm starting to be more aware of my relationship with Dad and can't understand his lack of interest and affection towards me. As I am a carbon copy of Mum, even down to her ginger hair and smile, she has passed on her neediness to me, maybe through the way I have been brought up. I don't get any love or affection from Reg, and the love I should have received from Mum is blighted by the fact that she is drinking.

So once again I look to Dad to love and comfort me. But no matter how hard I look, it is never there and, I start to realize, never will be, not in the way I want and need it. He hasn't been a bad dad to me – he just hasn't been a good one. In my eight-year-old way, I'm trying very hard to bridge the gap, but he never looks to meet me halfway and I give up. He either can't or won't do it.

There's another reason why I want and need this from my father. Things are getting much worse at home.

* * *

I'm finding it more and more difficult to cope with Reg's beatings. I just don't know when they're going to happen or why. They seem to occur without any obvious trigger and I'm always a bag of nerves when Mum isn't in the house.

My fear of Reg attacking me is as bad as the physical pain. At least with the beating, I know that once it's over it won't happen again that day. I will do anything to pacify Reg, but it doesn't seem to have any effect either way. If he *is* going to hit me, there's nothing I can do about it. I just have to look for the tell-tale signs – although that doesn't make much difference to my response, which is to do nothing and wait for the worst to happen. What I should do when I see him turn into a raging monster is to run out of the house. That would be the sensible thing to do. With a back and a front door it would be easy and there's no way he could catch me.

But I don't do this. I just stay there and wait for the blows to fall. When they do, I work out that he actually runs out of steam fairly quickly. By then, he will have punched me twenty times or so. But those punches are very different from before. The shock factor of being beaten has gone and I have become hardened to them. I won't cry out and don't cry so much afterwards.

Because of this, his punches are even more savage and powerful. It is as if he is trying to hit another adult. It hurts like hell but I'm not going to give him the satisfaction of seeing me cry. As before, I curl up into the tightest ball I can and wait for it all to stop. This coping strategy allows me to deal with the beatings. I don't want to be beaten but feel that I must have deserved it for some reason. After all, he is an adult and, more than that, the male influence in my life. Surely he must know what is best for me. I can't work out why he is doing it but that doesn't mean it isn't right. I assume the problem lies with me not him, so I just take it and I ask no questions. I don't even tell Mum.

How am I to know that my submissive nature is allowing me to accept beatings that I don't deserve or understand? How am I to know that Reg has completely abused his position of parental trust to treat me in this savage way?

As hard as the beatings are to cope with, something else happens which, as far as my life is concerned, is even more serious and dangerous. Mum is still drinking and now she's drinking more frequently – a subtle, important shift. When I come home from school nowadays, more often than not she has already started drinking and I've noticed that she has already prepared dinner for Reg and me, so that all she has to do is heat it up again. This way she doesn't have to start cooking from scratch when she is already starting to lose coordination.

She will usually sit and eat with us, but sometimes she disappears upstairs after she's served Reg and me our food, and by the time she reappears it's obvious to me at least that she is well on her way to getting smashed.

Occasionally she doesn't even bother to have any food prepared for us, and Reg and I will have to fix something up between us – beans or sardines on toast being a staple fallback – which we do sullenly, without speaking a word to each other, or only the minimum words necessary to get us through the meal – 'pass the salt', 'one slice or two?', 'hand me that glass', while Mum's quietly getting plastered upstairs. And sometimes it's not even that quietly.

I can sometimes hear her stumbling around upstairs in her room while we're downstairs eating. Her own meal-times become more erratic when she's drinking.

As the evening wears on, Reg struggles to contain her when she is drunk but once he's had enough, he goes to bed, leaving her to it. As always, she wanders clumsily around the house, until she eventually goes to bed herself and as before I have to lie in bed and listen out for her to make sure she is OK. I have previously found her asleep on the kitchen floor and can sense the danger she places herself in when she is drunk. But on those occasions, she has left me alone and not demanded that I touch her. I have assumed that this is something she is no longer inter-ested in; I have tried to lock that part of my life in a cupboard in my head forever.

If only that were the case.

I now have a proper bedroom with a proper bed, which is great because until only a few months ago I had to clamber over old bits of broken furniture and gardening tools to get into my camp bed. But it also means that Mum now has easy access to me.

* * *

I wake up in bed, jolted out of deep sleep. I assumed Mum was asleep too but now I can hear her … she's coming into my room and I know she's been drinking so much that she's virtually unconscious.

The light switch for my bedroom is outside my door. All of a sudden, the light comes on and the door is flung wide open. Mum is standing in the doorway, half naked. I blink in the blinding light and look forward.

'Mum, is that you?' I croak, my voice and head still half asleep.

'Yes, this is your mother,' she replies in a slow, stern, matronly drawl.

As I sit up in bed, trying to get my bearings, she lunges forward. She can't stand properly and the only thing that stops her falling over is my bed. She leans on the corner and looks at me with those same lifeless, glassy eyes I have seen so many times before when she is in this state.

In one swift movement, she grabs my blankets and yanks them off me and the bed, tossing them on the floor. Quick as a flash, I jump out of bed. I have seen Mum drunk enough times to know that this is probably not going to go away quickly and I don't want to be lying on the bed, no matter what is about to happen.

'What do you want, Mum?' I ask, hardly daring to ask the question.

'I want you to play with me, David,' she replies in a low, growly voice.

She lies down on the bed and spreads her legs in front of me.

I am shocked and horrified. I can scarcely believe what I am seeing and hearing. All the bad old memories of Calder Bridge come flooding back. A beating from Reg is bad enough but this is ten times worse and I thought it had gone away for good. I can hardly speak or respond and struggle to get my words out.

'B…but Mum, I don't want to,' I say, backing away.

'David,' she commands in an authoritative slur, 'come here now and do as you're told.'

So I do.

I go and stand at the side of my mother. I can smell the stench of brandy, and it makes me want to vomit. I can see Mum's naked body and even though I am used to seeing it when she is drunk, I always look somewhere else. But now I have no choice.

Mum takes my hand and puts it on her minnie. She rubs it around, while she lies there moaning.

It feels horrible and disgusting and I think I'm going to be sick.

Mum continues rubbing herself with my hand for just a few minutes then pushes it away. She has probably got bored. Her boredom threshold is very low when she is drunk.

I move back again, hoping and praying she won't ask me again. She doesn't and instead tries to get up. She falls out of my bed onto the floor, grabs my homework table to get herself to her feet and without saying a word, leaves the room, turning the light off after she slams shut the door.

I stand in the darkness and think about what has just happened. I know that what we have done is wrong but this is my mother and I am her son. I am meant to do as I am told and so I do.

I pick up my blankets and put them on my bed. Then I crawl underneath them, pulling them high over my head. I lie there wishing and praying that Mum doesn't come back to see me tonight.

***

She doesn't come back tonight but I somehow know that it won't be the last time she will come to visit me in my room. As a younger child, I dealt with it by thinking it was some kind of game but now, even though I'm not yet fully sexually aware, I know it means something completely different.

It causes me huge problems that I can't deal with. I have no-one to talk to or anyone who can tell me what to do. This is a difficult time for me and I keep looking for something positive to make it OK. And then on 30 April 1977, when I am nine, something happens that I think will change everything for the better: Reg and Mum get married.

It seems fantastic news when they tell me. Maybe this is our chance to become a proper family. It will bring the three of us closer together. We have been living with Reg for several years but this will take us to a new level. I am sure Reg will look at me in a different light once I am his legal stepson and Mum's visits to my bedroom will come to a stop.

On the big day, Mum looks amazing. She is dressed in a white outfit with a beautiful white hat. She is calm and serene, and enjoys the whole ceremony. It is held at Halifax Registry Office but to me it is as impressive as any church. Reg looks dapper in a black three-piece suit and proud as any husband could be marrying the woman he loves. They seem very happy and, despite the age gap, look like a couple well suited to each other. I'm wearing a brand new pair of trousers, shirt and tie, and for once Mum hasn't bought them secondhand. There are only a few people at the wedding but that doesn't matter. We have a fantastic meal at an expensive pub restaurant and the waiter can tell we've been to a wedding.

'My Mum and Grandad have just got married,' I say proudly, with a big smile on my face.

He looks slightly bewildered and everyone laughs.

We look great as a family together. Maybe this will be the start of a new chapter in our lives.

* * *

But of course it isn't all quite as I imagined. One day when Mum has started drinking early – but not yet drunk enough to be ragingly out of control – she is more candid than usual to me about her life with Reg and tells me that, because of his age, she has been feeling she needs to protect her future and getting married has been the only way to guarantee that she will get the house if he dies.

I'm certain that Reg and Mum love each other enough to want to celebrate their relationship by getting married. But she can be practical and quite ruthless too if necessary. While living with Reg, she has run the finances very well but if Reg dies and the house doesn't go to her for whatever reason, she knows it will leave her in a mess and she can't let that happen.

One of the things that probably worries her is the problem with Pauline, Reg's daughter, who lives with her family in the farm at the top of our lane. Something has happened to cause a split between our two families but I don't know what it is. I have tried asking both Mum and Reg but they won't talk about it and I know better than to ask again.

It's so serious that Reg has stopped speaking to his daughter or any of the family on the farm. Something tells me that it's all really about Mum. I think it's because they suspect she's trying to fleece Reg. After all, even I at the age of nine can see that many people wouldn't understand why a young, attractive woman would want to settle down with a fat, bald man, 35 years her senior.

The reality of course is quite different. When they met, although he had no mortgage, the house was in a bad state of disrepair. It was Mum that got it back together by going out to work full time and using her financial acumen to make the money go a very long way. This is what has allowed them to repair, refurbish, extend and improve the house and turn it into a home. Not only that, but Reg now also enjoys the kind of life he could never have expected as a retired man on a state pension. He travels a lot more than he did before and she makes sure he goes on the old folks' coach trips from the local community centre.

Reg is a working–class man from a different generation with simple tastes. Even so, he wants for nothing and Mum makes sure that he has everything he needs and more. He never has to pay a bill, go shopping, deal with his pension or sort out things in the house. As Reg has got older and more dependent on her, she is always there for him and never leaves his side.

Unfortunately, there's a price to pay for living with her, which may have been the reason for the split with Pauline – the drinking. I'm starting to see how Mum has a pattern of behaviour which occurs with a lot of people she meets, and with almost all of them it ends disastrously.

She will befriend someone, get to know them, and conversation will soon become much more personal. She finds it easy to talk about intimate topics, encouraging other people to reciprocate. Once she feels she knows them well enough, she will get their phone number and start calling them at home.

That's when the problems start. She doesn't mean to step over the line by phoning them at home. She likes to chat and when she makes a new friend she likes to chat a lot. At first, the home calls are perfectly reasonable conversations, friendly and good natured. The only problem is that she talks too long and she can be a handful to get off the phone. When I'm older and mates phone the house she will talk them to death as well.

'Your mother,' a friend of mine later comments with a grin, 'could talk a glass eye to sleep.'

One of Mum's friends puts it another way. If Mum ever rings up and his wife isn't there, she will talk to him instead and usually for some time.

'If your Mum ever phones,' he remarks affectionately, 'it will always be at the beginning of the rugby, and you know you'll be lucky if you get to see the second half.'

But Mum's legendary talking ability isn't a serious issue. Most people who speak to her can deal with it. The problems really start when she feels she can phone someone once she's drunk. After getting through drinking a whole bottle of brandy she will be completely drunk and unable to leave the house. In that state, she forgets how to act and treat people properly. Other people, even those who know her well, don't know just how badly she gets drunk because they never see it, but the phone gives her the chance to contact them. Once drunk, there are no barriers to what she might say. She'll talk about anything, no matter how inappropriate.

Some people can handle it and will be a sympathetic ear for her to vent her frustrations and opinions. Others find it increasingly difficult to get her off the phone which will make her angry and then she'll respond very badly. This may not happen in a single conversation but it usually does at some point with everyone she befriends. Her mood swings are highly volatile and unpredictable. One minute she can be chatting nicely, the next crying and looking for sympathy, then deeply and personally abusive.

This may have been what has caused the split between us and Reg's family. If they found out about her drinking, and she has been phoning them at all when she was drunk, that would have been enough for them to have deep concerns. I may never know exactly what the trigger was for this family split, but whatever it is, Reg's daughter and all her family are no longer speaking to us.

This must upset Reg – after all, these are his daughter and grandchildren who own and farm the fields around our house and are always working close to the house. Add to this the fact that the only practical way to their farm is up our lane and what it actually means is that Reg has a family he sees many times each day but who treat him as if he were invisible.

Mum has made the situation even more difficult. She isn't prepared to say sorry and she will never accept that she's in the wrong about anything. I often see her brow-beat Reg into submission on all kinds of issues and he knows better than to call her bluff or go behind her back. But what I know is that he genuinely loves her so much that he's prepared to turn his back on his own flesh and blood rather than lose her.

* * *

Reg's family aren't the only one to have an issue with their union. So does my real grandad – Mum's father. Because of the 35-year age gap between Reg and Mum, he is only one year younger than Grandad Fred. I am very fond of Grandad. Since Grandma Sandra's death nearly a dozen years ago in 1966, he has lived alone in a rented house in Chisendale, the village Mum was brought up in as a child.

Grandad is very popular in Chisendale. As he has a car and has driven all his life, he takes elderly people out shopping. He's well known and well liked. His dog Bessie has been our family pet since she was a puppy. Mum and Dad had Bessie originally, but then Grandad had asked for her. She's a placid Labrador cross and she and Grandad are inseparable. Bessie can tell the difference between ice-cream vans. Grandad buys an ice-cream every day for himself and Bessie but two ice-cream vans will come past with different tunes. When the first plays, Bessie won't move an inch but when the second plays, she barks and jumps up and down to alert her master.

Grandad has a cheeky smile and an engaging, mischievous personality. He will get a Wellington boot and put a dog biscuit in the bottom. Of course Bessie, in pursuit of the biscuit, ends up walking around with the welly on her head. Bessie gets the biscuit and then throws the welly off. We visit him regularly. Even though he lives on the side of a road, it's in a rural area and he takes us for walks in the meadows, naming the various plants and getting us to smell the flowers. He's taught me to play chess and although he's a great player himself, he's generous enough to say that I occasionally get him in a jam.

Last year I went to his house on his birthday, which was on Boxing Day. He always has a large group of people there, especially having so many brothers and friends in the village. The highlight for me was when he asked me to read a book out loud to the assembled crowd. This was a great honour for me and they clapped when I had finished. Grandad beamed with pride and so did I.

But I sometimes think there may be another side to Grandad than the one I see. I can't ever remember going with Reg to Grandad's house. I know Grandad disapproved of Mum marrying a man so many years older than her. Mum is a difficult woman to live with but Reg has stuck to the task and they have ended up with a strong marriage. Grandad can't see that and has never fully accepted them being together.

I can also see that Grandad can be quite strict and sharp-tongued with me when he needs to be.

'Just remember, young boy, I have a way with grandchildren,' he'll say if I ever test his patience, and the one time I dared to answer back, I immediately regretted it.

'Get upstairs, young Satan,' he boomed.

Mum sometimes repeats this story and it always seems very funny. But I've started to realize that if he can be so severe with his own grandson, he might have been much worse to Mum when she was growing up with him.

In May 1978, a month or so after my tenth birthday, I happen to find on the kitchen table a letter Grandad has written to Mum. It reads:

Dear Carol. My health has deteriorated somewhat in the past few days and I think you should keep in touch with me to the extent of phoning me a couple of times a week. Yours Dad.

Even though I'm still young I can see how strangely unemotional this letter is. It may be because Grandad comes from a generation who find it hard to wear their heart on their sleeve – but it still seems a curiously love-less way to write to your daughter when you know you don't have long to live.

A few months after this, Mum breaks the news to me: Grandad has died, before his 71st birthday in December. I cry, feeling the loss acutely. I miss our games of chess and walks in the meadows.

I go with Mum after his death to sort out his personal effects and we come across his diary. Every Saturday has a date in it – '5.30 T&J'. We don't know what this refers to and it isn't until weeks later, watching television, that the penny drops.

'That's it!' Mum shouts.

'That's what?' Reg asks.

'T&J stands for Tom and Jerry,' she says triumphantly.

Grandad had actually written down the time Tom and Jerry was on television so he wouldn't forget it. I'm glad that it was important to him to watch cartoons.

Other entries in his diaries are quotes, such as 'A pessimist looks at a glass of water as being half empty; the optimist as being half full.'

These kinds of messages intrigue me but I have no way of knowing at this age how important they are going to become to me at a much later period in my life. I do know, though, that Grandad will always be a special person in my life and I'm sad that he's died.

6

Interlude

Looking back on my childhood I've got no idea what effect Grandad's death had on Mum. She always mentioned her mother's birthday every year to me but never her father's. As his birthday was Boxing Day it was easy to remember but she never mentioned it from the day he died and I'll never know what relationship Mum really had with her dad.

Grandad was a strong character. He certainly seemed to have wanted his kids to succeed. And that's just what Mum's brother, my Uncle Jim, did – he succeeded with a vengeance. But not Mum. Maybe the difference between his two children resulted in more pressure on Mum and maybe he treated her differently from Jim. That could have been the reason why she ended up hooked on drink and drugs once she left home.

I've heard a few suggestions at different times, both from friends and family, that Grandad may have sexually abused her. I have no way of knowing whether this was true, but if it was, did she think the things she made me do to her in the night were – in her drunken way of looking at things – 'normal' because they were also done to her?

Or maybe living in the shadow of a gifted older brother opened up a flaw in her make-up that made her do the terrible things she did to me. But all this guesswork doesn't explain why her brother also spent all his adult life addicted to drink and dying early.

I don't know if my grandparents did something that created the problems that Mum and Uncle Jim went through and I never will. Grandad died at the early age of 70. But something happened in the way he brought up his children that left behind not just one but two people who went through life creating destruction, turmoil and pain.

Some of the things Dad has told me as an adult have helped me slot together some important pieces in the jigsaw of Mum's early life. Her difficulties started in her teenage years. Even before she started drinking she had drug problems. In 1963, at the age of 18, she began her nurse training in a Halifax hospital and would take drugs on the ward when working night shifts. This may have just been to help keep her awake, but it created some kind of dependency.

Then in June 1966, during the finals of her nursing exams, her mother died. Mum was only 21 and although she qualified as a nurse in February 1967, and nursed during her three years' training, she never took up nursing after she qualified. At the time of her mother's death, my parents were seeing each other and married a few months later, in November 1966.

Dad says that at the time of the wedding, he knew nothing of Mum's personal demons – throughout her life she was clever at hiding them – including the drink and drugs which only emerged after they were married. I think he must have discovered just how bad things were very quickly, and although he is reluctant to talk about this period, on the rare occasions that he does, he relates incidents that defy belief.

On one occasion before I was born, Mum was so high on drugs or alcohol that she ran naked down the street in Calder Bridge. Dad chased after her and only caught her when a kindly gentleman stopped her and looked after her until he arrived.

After she finished nursing she no longer had access to the drugs she craved. But back then it was common practice for local surgeries to put out repeat-prescription drugs on the counter for patients to pick up. Because she knew what the drugs were, she used to steal them. In a small village it was inevitable that she would eventually get caught, but until she did, she would take them and use them at home.

This was astonishing behaviour for anyone, but especially for my mother. She had a strict moral upbringing by her parents and throughout my childhood she regularly attended the local Methodist church.

Although as a child I always went with her to church, there was no real sense of religion at home. We didn't say grace or prayers – it was simply a matter of going to church on Sunday. But I knew that church was important to her – it seemed to be one place where she could feel that sense of peace she so badly needed.

But although she would have had to wrestle very hard with her conscience, to bring her to the point of stealing anything – let alone drugs – the demons in her reduced her to that state.

Her behaviour devastated Dad. He was and is one of the most placid, easy-going people I know but when he speaks about living with her, he does so with gravity and deep sorrow. When one day recently I asked him about his marriage to my mother, he looked down, paused and shook his head. As he looked up his eyes were glistening with the sadness and pain of 35-year-old memories.

'David, I cannot say. They were terrible things, just terrible.'

* * *

Although she rarely talked about her childhood, a picture begins to form in my mind of her family background. I know that Mum had good but strict parents. They were married in 1933 so they were nearly twelve years into the marriage when Mum was born in 1945. By that time they had already had one other child, Mum's brother Jim, so they probably knew a thing or two about how to bring up their children. I never knew her mother, Sandra Stones, but I recently met someone who worked with her forty years ago in the public library in Chisendale where my grandmother was born and raised. She described my gran as happy-go-lucky – cheerful, merry, maybe even a little impulsive. The same person told me how she doted on both her children, my mother and her older brother, Jim. She constantly bought gifts for them and talked about them in the way mothers do about their children. This went on even when Mum was older and had met my father.

My mother's father Fred was more of a disciplinarian. His job involved collecting insurance payments from people's houses. He was an intelligent man, a highly respected local chess player who played correspondence chess with up to forty opponents at once. His job didn't stretch him at all, but he was happy doing it and turned down promotion many times. Fred came from a family of seven brothers, all of whom were very bright but who performed working-class jobs through choice. They had opportunities to progress but chose not to do so because of an almost puritanical streak that ran through that side of the family.

A good example was when one of my grandfather's brothers got the chance of a lifetime. He was working in a mill when he won a scholarship to Oxford. This was a huge opportunity for a working-class lad from the north of England in the 1920s. He duly went up to Oxford, completed his degree and then, incredibly, returned to his home town and to the mill where he had previously worked, because he didn't believe he should profit from his intelligence.

Mum's elder brother, Jim, was a clever, gifted man. He won lots of award in school, including Victor Ludorum as best student of the year, took the lead in the school play, ran with the local Harriers, and even set a school record of 95% in his O-level Maths exams. As a young man Jim was good-looking, charming, funny, quick with his tongue and had the world at his feet. Sandra, my grandmother, fiercely protective over her children, wrote to the Oxford admissions tutor claiming that class discrimination had barred him from gaining a place at university. What's more, she had her letter and the very weak unconvincing reply printed in the local paper.

In one crucial way, though, Jim differed from his father and uncles. He used his intelligence and abilities to make himself wealthy by going into mining engineering. To complete his mining degree, he did a stint in Ghana. By the time he returned from Africa, he was drinking a bottle of whisky a day. He was only in his early twenties and despite all his obvious talents and opportunity he continued to drink ferociously the rest of his life. He died at the early age of 49, not of an alcohol-related disease but of cancer. He didn't leave a will despite his wealth and six children from three marriages. He must have known the problems and pain that this would cause and so it seems an oddly thoughtless thing for a bright, intelligent man to do.

Apart from Jim and Mum there was no history of excessive drinking on my maternal grandparents' side of the family. I sensed, though, that Mum lived in her brother's shadow when they were growing up. Jim was almost a perfect son in every way – sociable, popular, intelligent, an athlete, a dramatist, a record-breaking student. Mum was nowhere near as bright as him. Her facility with the English language, both written and spoken, was flawless, but otherwise her academic abilities were way behind Jim's. Yet if having him as a brother caused her any emotional issues it didn't explain why Jim also came to have an alcohol problem.

The dark side of Mum's character meant severe consequences for those who crossed her. Alcohol produced such a complete personality shift that I believe she had no idea what she was doing. That was one of the main reasons why I never told her what happened between us – she simply had no recollection of the night before. When sober, she couldn't keep anything to herself – she just had to blurt it out – and I find it impossible to imagine her knowing what happened when she was drunk and never mentioning it.

There were so many 'mornings after' when I wanted to say something to Mum about what went on between us the night before, but I never dared. Life with Mum just seemed so different in the daylight that I could never bring myself to mention the unmentionable, even sometimes doubting the evidence of my own memory and senses.

The only way I could live with this conflict was to accept that my Light Mummy had no awareness of my Dark Mummy and that if the two were ever to meet the consequences would be unimaginable. It's also the reason why only a handful of people knew about it until I decided to write this book and until now nobody has known the whole truth.

7

Fair Game

At the age of eleven and in my last year at junior school, I am still very well behaved in class and only occasionally get into trouble, like the time when I was nine when I said 'knickers' to a teacher. I don't think it was the worst insult in the world, but even so, I ended up having to stand in the hall, waiting for the headmaster to return. When he did, he banged his bike helmet on my head a few times and I cried my eyes out.

I have done well academically. In my last two years at my junior school I've come second in both years out of the whole school. I am pleased and so is Mum, which makes it even better: anything that pleases her is good. She pushes me to read every day but apart from that she believes in leaving me to it. She makes me do my homework though, and my attendance had also been excellent. In my final two years at junior school, 1977–79, I have had 100% attendance; the year before I missed just two days. I have to be on my deathbed to miss a day.

I'm not a natural at sports but, like most boys, I desperately want to play and be part of the team. On a couple of occasions I've played for the school football team and acquitted myself well, showing that I'm an eager, hard-working player, if not exactly overflowing with talent.

At Christmas I got a fantastic surprise. Several pupils in my class had the chance to go to my teacher's house one evening to help make buns for the Christmas party. Names were drawn out of a hat and my name was drawn. I was beside myself with excitement. After school, the chosen few went up to Mrs Greenham's house in Calder Bridge – a large modern bungalow with spectacular patio windows that look down over the valley. She is a slim, attractive woman who stunned us once by showing us a photo of her breastfeeding. Her husband owns a sewing shop only fifty yards from where we used to live in the four houses next to the scrapyard. I haven't visited Calder Bridge very much since we moved to Ludden Vale so going there felt strange. It brought back memories from the bad old days and reminded me of how they had now returned. But the evening was still a great success.

At home, though, life is getting steadily worse. Reg has now taken to kicking as well as punching me. It's as though he's learning to pace himself, and is even taking a kind of professional pride in his work which, as always, only takes place when Mum is out of the house. As much as I dread those long nights when she's drinking, I dread even more the times when she leaves me alone with Reg. I'll try to find excuses to leave the house myself, but Reg seems to be watching and waiting for me, ready to pounce on me like a cat lunging at a mouse.

Nowadays when he assaults me, he is able to go on much longer than he used to when he was only punching me. He's careful not to kick me so hard as to injure me, but the combined effect of this barrage of vicious punches and kicks is to weaken my body and crush my spirit. On these occasions, after Reg has finished his strenuous workout on me, I remain in my bedroom long after he has returned downstairs, and even when Mum has arrived back home I stay in my room.

Curiously, when Reg has 'taught me a lesson', as he still likes to put it, Mum never calls me downstairs. Or maybe she does but I'm hurting too much to notice; I'm too miserable and demoralized, and too weak to move. I eventually climb into bed and cry myself to sleep and at these times, perhaps mercifully, I have no idea whether Mum might be crashing around in her room on one of her benders.

But even this is about to change. I have assumed that there's no way I would be abused on the same night by both my mother and my stepdad. That assumption is to be challenged before very long.

* * *

I'm now 11 and starting to look at girls differently. I know several boys in my year who already have girlfriends, but none of the girls ever normally gives me a second look. I do think about them sometimes though, and one day I ask a girl to come out with me to the cinema in Ludden Bridge. Her name is Sally Seymour; she has long brown hair, and although she's a little demure and standoffish, I think she's the most beautiful girl in the world. A lot of boys fancy her and the fact that she's prepared to go to see a movie with me is amazing.

We have a fabulous day. She comes to my house to eat first and then we go to the cinema. The film is *Superman* −

the blockbuster movie of summer 1979. As we sit there in the dark I imagine that I'm Clark Kent and that Sally is Lois Lane and that she'll discover who I really am after I rescue her from the deadly peril awaiting her outside in Ludden Bridge. Then she'll realize that I am actually Superman – tall, lithe and handsome with an amazing physique, a fantastic brain and incredible memory – and of course, just like Christopher Reeve, witty, kind and considerate into the bargain. I'll be the envy of all the boys in school and so will she.

I can't wait to see her at school on the following Monday. But as soon as I see her after the weekend, Sally tells me she doesn't want to be my girlfriend any more.

I am devastated.

I know this happens all the time to millions of kids but rejection hits me hard. In the next few years, when future girlfriends finish with me – which for a long time they do – I continue to take the rejection very personally. I think I must be too clingy or something. I don't know what it is. Maybe girls think I'm not charming enough or that I'm lacking personality, though sometimes this isn't the case and then I can suddenly feel on top of the world.

I know I'm basically very likeable and when I'm in the right mood I can get other kids laughing at my jokes. It's just that I don't have any real sense of being popular and having a lot of friends. Friends come and go and somehow I don't feel close to anyone, which is what I really want, Maybe I'm also paranoid about not being good looking and having ginger hair – and of course I still have a lisp, which doesn't help.

* * *

Life changes dramatically for me when I start at Ludden High School in September 1979.

From being the oldest in school to being the youngest forces me to grow up quickly. I like some elements a great deal – the size of the school, the number of people – and in my first end-of-term report I receive praise for my keen attitude to my studies. Seeing children so much older than me lets me into a world I never knew existed. I like the hustle and bustle, the energy of the place.

School dinners are my favourite time. Most of the kids knock them because of soggy veg and poor quality food but I'm used to a cheap, basic diet at home so it's nice to have something different. I like to go in last and hang around for seconds.

But there are things about school I don't like. Even more than before I feel a huge need to conform and blend into the background. I don't want to be different in any way. But immediately I *am* singled out as being different when our lack of money at home pops up as a problem in the first few weeks.

School blazers are compulsory schoolwear but Mum doesn't have enough money to buy one at the beginning of my first school term. She is used to buying my clothes secondhand but it's virtually impossible to find a used blazer. So she sends a note to school, explaining that she'll be getting me one soon. Needless to say, every boy in my year has a school blazer apart from me. Not only that, but they all have 'normal' blue school jumpers and blue cotton shirts, the kind you buy from specialist schoolwear shops. But Mum won't go there unless she absolutely has to.

My first school photo, taken a few weeks after I've started at Ludden High, shows me wearing a secondhand jumper with some strange kind of knitwear weave to it, a grey nylon shirt and no blazer. The only thing I have that is new and the same as everyone else is my tie. I hate being the centre of attention yet I stick out like a sore thumb. People have cottoned on fairly quickly that we don't have much money, especially as I also have free school dinners, and I am ribbed relentlessly. Not having money has never bothered me before and on almost every level it doesn't now, except at school. I just want to be the same as everyone else. My goofy teeth and ginger hair don't help.

On one occasion Lauren, one of the most popular girls in the class, comes up to me just as the class is breaking up for lunch.

'Hiya, David, are you alright?' she asks.

'I'm fine,' I reply warily, wondering what's coming next.

Lauren is gorgeous. She has money which she uses to dress very trendily, making her popular with the girls, and she is also classically good looking. Every boy at school fancies her. We are poles apart and she would never normally speak to me. As soon as she does, everyone turns and looks to see what's going on. The whole class is watching.

'Can you do a favour for me, please?' she asks sweetly.

'Of course,' I reply, relieved that it's a favour, not some stunt to show me up.

'Can you say the following phrase, just for me?'

'Sure.'

'She sells seashells on the seashore.'

I repeat the sentence back to her and the whole class falls about laughing. Every word with 's' in it comes out wrong and I look like a fool. I'd love to say that I laugh with them and manage to shrug it off easily. But I just want the ground to swallow me up. It may only be a tiny incident – after all, it's hardly major bullying, just a harmless poke at a kid in class – but it brings back memories of being bullied by Karen, the older girl in my first year at junior school, at the age of five. It makes me feel silly and stupid and weaker than the others.

There is a hierarchy of students, even within my year, and I am somewhere down at the bottom, looking up at the rest. Those at the top impose themselves and take advantage of the rest of us. It isn't even as if I want to be at the top. I just want to blend into the wallpaper and drift along unnoticed.

But that's not how it works. At school if you have a more submissive nature than the average child, which I do, then it's difficult to control what's happening around you. Having ginger hair makes it even worse. Only a tiny percentage of people have it and it's a social nightmare. All the lads love girls with red hair but girls actively shy away from boys who have it. As an adult, it has always amazed me how it's socially acceptable to say certain things about people with ginger hair that would be considered downright offensive if aimed at people who are black or gay.

I am fair game to everyone and hate having red hair. It doesn't help when a few weeks later a new battery comes out and there is a huge advertising campaign. One boy, who is well known as a bully in the year above me, is the first to catch on to the slogan. He is passing the football courts one day when I'm watching the lads in my year play football.

'Oi ginger!' he shouts.

Everyone looks at us as if they think something's about to kick off.

'You're just like a Duracell battery,' he smiles, 'the one with the copper-coloured top.'

Everyone laughs. Even I think it's funny, but the problem is, they're laughing *at* me, not *with* me. Digs about having a lisp or ginger hair are not major bullying issues. In fact, I actually suffer very little physical intimidation at school. But I have inherited Mum's hypersensitivity to criticism and can't easily shrug them off.

The situation at school is magnified for me because I have no-one to turn to at home. I would love a dad who could take me to one side and teach me to look after myself. It would be so cool to learn witty replies to put down the piss-takers. And even better if someone could show me how to look after myself physically if I got into a fight.

Like all schoolboys, I get into the occasional scrape which I always lose. There's one lad, much bigger than me, who regularly imposes himself upon me physically. Being in my class means that I see a lot of him and he's known as a bully. He doesn't go all out to hurt me but just to push me around. He'll tip my bag out; shove me in the back. Many days I wish I could defend myself against him. At the very least, it would be nice to learn how to respond to these types of situations.

Ironically, although Reg has been beating me at home for a long while, this isn't helping me learn how to defend myself. Because he is an adult, I have learned how to do the opposite: take a beating and get up afterwards. And as far as looking after me is concerned, Reg really doesn't care any more. He leaves every decision about me to Mum. His interest and impact on my life now seem to be virtually nil. It's a combination of his age – he's now over 70 –

and the fact that he genuinely can't be bothered. Now I'm at secondary school, his attitude is like that of a distant relative who happens to be living in the same house as me. He has grandchildren older than me and, after all, he was bringing up his own children years ago and doesn't have the energy or inclination to do it all over again with me.

Dad certainly isn't around to give me guidance on this either. He has effectively removed himself from my life. Overnight, this has been reinforced for me when he rings to say that he has decided to emigrate with Maureen and her children to the States. There is no discussion about this: I haven't been involved in the decision-making process at all. It is a fait accompli and I have to accept it.

In retrospect, as an adult, I have no issue with Dad emigrating to the US. He was trying to better himself and make the most of his life. He felt that the opportunities coming his way in the States were too big to turn down. I'm proud of my dad that he was prepared to put himself out on a limb and take such a risky, life-changing decision when it would have been easier to stay put and make the most of his considerable skills in the UK. I now believe that life isn't a dress rehearsal and his decision to emigrate was courageous. From conversations I've had with him since, I know that Dad genuinely felt he was leaving me behind in a stable, loving family environment. But he couldn't have been more wrong.

Yet even if Dad and Reg have shrugged off their parental responsibilities, Mum could have filled the void they left if she chose to do so – and she does to a certain extent. She is keen on my schooling and health, and one thing she does for me that I will always be grateful for is to sort out my lisp, which is due to my having too many teeth. She pushes for the dentist to deal with it. A couple of teeth removed and a brace fitted for a short while banish my lisp and goofy teeth forever.

But she is still coming to my room at night for her Special Time. I have no choice but to go along with it but it's tearing me apart. And to make matters worse, I'm already hurting badly when she comes.

* * *

He goes for me minutes after I arrive home from school, almost like he's been waiting to do it all afternoon. I've made the mistake of asking him if there was still any tea in the pot.

'I'll give you tea,' he explodes. 'I'll give you bloody tea. What do you think I am, your skivvy!'

In the next second, before I can escape upstairs, he's onto me, smashing his fist into my stomach. As I collapse on the hall floor, doubled up in agony, Reg begins kicking me in the backside.

'I didn't mean anything, Grandad, honest I didn't!' I sob.

'Don't answer me back, you little brat!' he storms, and I can hear him breathing heavily as he continues to kick me. 'I know your game. I'll teach you to cheek me!'

By the time Reg is through with me, I feel like how I imagine a victim of a very bad car crash might feel – if they were unlucky enough to be still conscious. Sobbing and winded, I limp slowly and painfully up to my bedroom and stagger into my bed.

* * *

As I lie there, smarting and bruising from Reg's beating, I don't know how much more I can take, but what can I do?

I can hardly say anything to Mum. I'm sure that her emotional state is too fragile to cope with discovering what Reg has been doing to me. But I'm now so confused that I'm even starting to wonder whether Mum might be in cahoots with Reg. After all, I'm just as much a victim of her unhappiness and rage as I am of his.

I haven't been downstairs since he left my room. I am aching and all I want to do is sleep.

Suddenly I can hear her at my door. She switches my bedroom light on from outside the room, then flings the door open, rushing in and pulling my bedclothes off in one swift movement. I jump out of bed and she lies down on it. I stand on one side in the shadows, in the naïve hope that she won't notice me. Of course, this never happens.

'David, come and play with me,' she instructs.

'But, Mum, I don't want to do it,' I whine.

'Just get over here and do it now!'

I shuffle across the room slowly, knowing her attention span and boredom threshold are very low. I figure the slower I walk, the greater the chance she will lose interest before I get there and stagger off somewhere else in the house.

Once by the side of the bed, she grabs my hand and places it on her vagina. I deliberately play with her in a way that I know will not actually cause her any pleasure. I hope this may discourage her from asking me again in the future. But it only makes her angry. She grabs my hand, trying to make me do it the way she likes it. But I still resist doing it this way and try and make the whole thing more difficult.

I know that there's a risk for me in doing so. If I'm lucky she may get bored with trying to make me do it properly and give up, in which case the whole episode will be over pretty quickly.

On the other hand, a much worse outcome is that because I'm not doing it properly, she won't get enough satisfaction from it. In that case it can last much longer as she's trying to reach some kind of satisfaction before she stops – sometimes a lot longer.

By now, resisting Mum isn't an option, even though my instinct is still to resist whenever she smashes the door open. I'm old enough to know this is all wrong. It makes me feel uncomfortable and sick to the point of nausea.

She's asking me to do things a child should never have to do to their mother and I'm seeing her in a condition which beggars belief. She's drunk but, more than that, she's turned into a monster, using language I never hear her use when sober, especially if I resist her.

'David, come over here.'

'No, Mum, I'm not coming over.'

'Fucking hell, David, can't you just do as you're shitting told!'

She's semi-naked, wearing just a T-shirt or jumper. I don't want to see any part of her naked at any time, particularly not her bottom half. I wonder why she dresses like this. Sometimes she's completely naked if she's got undressed for bed and decides to visit me.

When she's finally finished with me for the night she leaves the room and goes downstairs. All I want to do now is stay under the covers. I desperately want to take refuge in sleep and forget what has just taken place with my mother and what happened earlier with my stepfather.

I just want it all to end – but the nightmare is still not over.

Now I can hear her in the kitchen. I know she wants to cook. If I don't follow her downstairs to the kitchen, she might burn herself or worse.

When I get downstairs Mum is already trying to use the cooker. I can't make her see that this is a bad idea or that she should have a bun or a cake or something that doesn't need cooking. I wait with her while she fumbles around the kitchen making a horrible mess.

Now she's spilling food and oil all over the kitchen and she's trying to light the gas cooker with matches. As so many times before, I can't help myself. I have to try to go to her aid – to stop her setting fire to the kitchen – but when I start to move towards her, she freaks, swinging for me and punching me square in my face when I get within range.

She's even throwing food and pans at me, not caring if she hits me, or the damage she causes.

So I retreat and go and sit in the next room, leaving the sliding door open so that I can sneak a look through. That way, she won't see me watching her, but I can keep an eye and ear on what she's doing.

I sit and wait, watching out for her. The night drags on. She's now been in the kitchen trying to cook food for over an hour.

Eventually she gives up. I don't know whether she's cooked anything after all this time but the result of her efforts are littered all over the cooker, and now that she's finished cooking, getting her to bed is the next hurdle – and it's a huge one.

The biggest challenge is helping her upstairs without receiving a smack in the teeth. As they are stone steps she slips and catches her legs which are, as usual, covered in multicoloured bruises. Getting within arm's length means risking another punch in the face so I walk behind her, letting her climb under her own steam and stopping her from falling if she loses her balance.

Once upstairs, she makes her own way to her room and puts herself to bed. I return to my room, remake my bed and turn off the light.

The fear of what might happen is often worse than what does happen. Sometimes, it's almost as bad not getting woken up. Lying in bed, after she has supposedly gone to sleep, I wait in the dark, praying she won't come back. I can lie awake for ages after she's gone to bed, listening to hear her stir. Eventually, I fall asleep through sheer exhaustion.

* * *

The worst aspect of the relationship is the role reversal. Despite all her drink problems, Mum runs a pretty tight ship when sober. She controls me with an iron rod, sometimes too strongly. But she always knows where I am makes sure I come to no harm. I don't have to think things through because Mum makes it crystal clear how I should act and the consequences if I don't. If there is a problem at school she is in touch straightaway; and on the rare occasions when I get detention, she investigates why it has happened. As a weak-willed child I need that kind of guidance from a parent. I am told what to do and when to do it, and I do it.

But this all changes when she's drunk. I haven't forgotten the nasty experience of her hitting me in the face after I found her asleep on the kitchen floor. On that occasion I had a bruise just below my left eye for several days. But just like with the bruises Reg gives me, Mum seems to turn a blind eye to them: she will still make sure I brush my teeth and comb my hair, but she doesn't comment on any signs on my face or body of any kind of physical assault, and nor does anyone at school. I sometimes feel like the walking wounded, and yet no one offers to help.

I need support but although I'm still not even a teenager I'm the one who's having to do all the supporting. From now onwards, I know it's up to me to ensure that Mum remains safe if she wants to cook when drunk. She is coming to me for physical contact at night but I still don't want her to come to any harm. So our roles have reversed, with me taking on a parental role. It is tiring, distressing and time-consuming.

At times, I want to leave her to it and go to bed but my conscience won't let me. Besides, there is no-one else. In spite of the beatings he is still giving me, Reg is too old to be up to the mental and physical battering Mum hands out on these occasions, so I have no choice but to shoulder the burden. It is all down to me.

The effect on me of this role reversal is devastating and my sleep is getting shot to pieces. Being woken up in the most dramatic fashion, by turning the light on when you're fast asleep, is a useful skill if you're a fireman, but not when you're a kid.

Around this time I start sleepwalking. I don't know if this has been triggered by these incidents with Mum, but for the rest of my life I will occasionally sleepwalk. It's usually triggered by stress or when I'm in a place I don't feel happy in.

I am now an unhappy 12-year-old, and my mental state is like a pressure-cooker with the lid screwed tight on, about to blow. I have no-one to confide in, no-one to ask the questions that are constantly on my mind:

Why does my mother drink so much?
Why does she come to me when she is drunk?
Why does she ask me to do the horrible things that she does?
What has made her turn to drink in the first place?

The questions keep on coming; the pressure keeps on growing, and I feel more and more frustrated and angry. As I get older, an inner rage quietly starts to build that will eventually explode in the most powerful and bizarre way.

* * *

My paternal grandmother is still going strong and as Dad has now emigrated to the States, it is down to Mum to take me to see her. I do this regularly, which I really like because she is such an interesting woman.

Eventually I go to see her on my own. Mum is never keen to drive me to and from Grandma's but she'll give me the bus fare. Grandma lives two bus rides away, which means going into town to change buses, so it's a real adventure.

Arriving at her house I enter her parallel universe. She has always been way off-centre, and it becomes even more apparent the older she gets. Her house is never exactly inviting these days. She now has iron bars at the window and multiple locks on the doors. Inside, it's dimly lit, giving a fortress-like feel to the place. Her eccentric lifestyle extends to her unorthodox views and interests, from the paranormal to meditation and spiritualism and she is only too happy to share her ideas with me. Some are harmless but others – such as the occult – I am definitely not going to learn about in school because they are patently unsuitable for children.

On one trip to Grandma's she gives me two books on Transcendental Meditation and magic – neither of which are exactly suitable reading material for a young impressionable kid. I read them on the bus going home and find them fascinating. Mum is only too aware of Grandma's eccentricities but is still happy for me to visit her. However, she always vets me when I return to see what she has given me.

'How were things at Grandma's?' she asks.

'Yeah, everything was fine. Grandma was well. We had some tea there,' I reply, hoping she won't notice the bag I am carrying.

'Did she give you anything?' she asks, furtively giving me the once over.

'No,' I lie, 'nothing at all.'

'Well, what's in the bag then?'

'Er, nothing, just some sweets, Mum.'

Of course, I'm not very adept at lying or hiding the forbidden books. Once she sees what they are about, she immediately confiscates them.

'Oh, Mum, can't I keep the books?' I plead.

'No, you can't,' she says decisively.

I know better than to argue: it will get me nowhere fast and just cheese her off. But it's too late anyway, I have already read the book on TM and immediately go up to my room to try and raise myself above my bed.

It doesn't work.

On another visit, Grandma gives me some Mars bars to take home. Mars is my favourite and I open them as soon as possible on the bus as I can't wait until I get home. As I undo the wrappers, the gorgeous chocolate I am expecting doesn't materialize. Instead, a pile of musty-smelling powder runs through my fingers onto the floor. Unbelievably, when I check the sell-by-date, the Mars bars should have been eaten over 12 months ago – at the latest. As chocolate already has a long sell-by-date, Grandma must have had it for several years before giving it to me, her only grandchild.

Although Grandma is undoubtedly weird, the real challenge for me is coming from much closer to home. The continued nocturnal visits from my mother, the ambivalence and physical abuse coming from Reg, the strangely detached attitude of my father are all turning my life into a cauldron of anxiety.

It feels like there's no-one I can turn to. I am isolated, lonely and things are happening that make me deeply unhappy and that I can't explain. Add to that the fact that adolescence is just around the corner, and that I have no friends to confide in, and I am just a big accident waiting to happen.

And it is about to, in an explosive way.

PART 2

Rage to Forget

8

Teenage Blues

I'm 13 but Reg is still using me as a punchbag. He shows no interest in me at any other time other than to vent his frustrations on me. As I don't have the personality to fight back or defend myself I continue to take it.

The last time Reg loses his temper with me, I can see it coming a mile off and, as always, I dash through the house up the stairs to my bedroom. This allows me to get as far away from him as possible, hoping that Reg, now an elderly man, will run out of steam before reaching me. It never happens so I don't know why I think this. Once he gets to me, he will be panting for breath but it never stops the beating.

On this occasion, Reg sets off in pursuit as usual. I get to the top of the stairs, look over the banister, see him coming upstairs and am about to open the door to my bedroom, when something stirs inside me. Suddenly I can't take this anymore.

'*Leave me alone, just leave me alone – don't come near me, don't you come near me!*' I scream from the top of the stairs over and over again. It doesn't sound like me but now I've started I can't stop. Something has flipped in me.

I don't expect Reg to stop. He will carry on up the stairs and beat me as usual. But incredibly he doesn't. Instead his face turns pale and he stops dead in his tracks. As I shout he turns around and walks back down and goes back into the kitchen.

I'm shocked into silence. For a moment I wonder whether I should go downstairs and see if he's all right. I start to creep down the stairs and then I hear something coming from behind the closed kitchen door.

It may be my imagination but it sounds like sobbing – or is it heavy breathing?

Maybe I've given him a heart attack by shouting at him like that. I have no idea what happens when you have a heart attack and what might bring it on. Then I decide not to tempt fate. And anyway, if he did have a heart attack, he'd deserve it.

Even so, I'm relieved an hour later when Mum comes home and I hear them talking downstairs quite normally as if nothing has happened.

And that's that. From this point onwards, Reg never lays a finger on me again.

But I cannot forget the pain he has inflicted on me, and the fact that to me he is a nasty, vicious bully. His beatings have been psychological as well as physical. He has never apologized afterwards or even acknowledged that he has done these things to me. But then one day, only a few weeks after Reg's beatings have come to an abrupt end, Mum makes an astonishing admission.

We're sitting, just me and Mum, at a trestle table in the garden. It's a beautiful sunny day in early June and I'm helping her shell peas which I love to do. I can smell the sweetness of the peas as they burst out of the pods and I can't resist eating one or two in every pod. Sometimes I pull too hard on the peas and crush them.

'Gently, David. Just let the peas out gently, like this.'

She shows me. With the slightest movement of her fingers she releases the peas so they plop out undamaged into the collecting bowl.

'And if you don't watch out,' she adds, 'we won't have any peas left the rate you're putting them away.'

'Sorry, Mum, I just can't help it. Anyway, I need building up.'

'Don't talk daft. And what about Reg – he needs building up more than you do. He's not getting any younger and I'm worried about him. He's not been himself for the last few weeks.'

I look up at Mum and I'm thinking about Reg's near miss of a heart attack. Does she know?

She's on to me instantly

'What's up, David? Is there something you're not telling me?'

'It's nothing, Mum.'

'Oh yes? Pull the other one. I'll find out anyway from Reg. He always tells me everything.'

I can't help it. I make a noise halfway between a chuckle and a snort.

'What?' says Mum.

I take a deep breath. It's now or never.

'Tells you everything! Did he tell you he nearly had a heart attack a few weeks ago when he was just about to beat me up.'

'What are you talking about?'

'Beat me up, like he's been doing for years. With his fists.'

'David, I—'

'I'm sorry, Mum,' I plough on. 'I didn't want to tell you, 'cos I knew you'd be upset, but it's true. He always does it when you're out and he usually makes sure he doesn't leave bruises where they'll show. He's been beating me up all this time and I didn't want you to know.'

I'm getting upset very quickly and if I carry on I know I'll start crying. I can't believe I'm telling her all this. Suddenly, now, out of nowhere, it's all coming out, and if I carry on I know I won't be able to stop, and that I will say everything, including the thing that's remained the biggest secret of all, unspoken between us for all these years.

'David, I know,' she says quietly.

'What do you mean?'

'Do you think I'm stupid? Of course I've known what's been going on between you and Reg for a long time. But what can I do? He must have his reasons and, after all, you can sometimes be a handful. I might not agree with his methods but your dad's not around and Reg is. And if that's how he's chosen to deal with you … well, maybe sometimes boys need a firm hand and you've just got to learn to take it.'

She purses her lips as if to say, *And that's all there is to be said about it.*

I am speechless. Stunned. My own mother is telling me that all this time she has known what's been going on – with Reg hitting and kicking me as though I were a cross between a punchbag and a football, and doing it whenever he felt like it, but she has chosen to do nothing about it. I'm shocked to the core. I can't understand any of it – can't imagine how any mother could know that such a thing was going on and do nothing.

For some reason I can't look at her any more. In any case Mum's now had her say and has clammed up completely. I know that's the last word from her on the subject and there's no room for further discussion.

I'm still holding a pod of peas. The shell is open and the peas are inside, lined up in a row like innocent children and I can't bring myself to break any more of them out of their shells. I lay the pod down on the table, run out of the garden and retreat into the house, leaving Mum to shell the rest of the peas on her own.

Lying on my bed with the sun shining outside, I try to make sense of it all.

I am now living three different lives, performing three different roles.

I'm still a young boy, under the care and protection of my mother and stepfather and sometimes, even now, I can still allow myself to be that person.

I'm also a target, an object, a waste bin, into which my mother and stepfather can empty out all their rubbish whenever they feel like it. They take out all their demons on me.

And now I'm also Mum's carer. I'm having to be like a father to her, just as she's like a mother to my stepdad.

I feel betrayed, let down. Reg is more important to her than her own son. The more I think about her and Reg the more upset I get. But deep down part of me can just about understand why she has allowed Reg to carry on doing what he's done to me. She found someone who wanted to take her on with all her problems and she wasn't about to give that up. Even if it meant knowing that he was beating up her own son at home when she wasn't there.

I'm suddenly struck with a chilling thought. Maybe she does know what she's doing to me when she is drunk and, for that reason, she doesn't see much wrong with what Reg has been doing. I can't or don't want to believe this possibility but how else can I explain her failure to protect me like a mother should? This is too awful to think about. I go downstairs, get out my bike and head out into the late afternoon. I don't know where I'm going, just anywhere, away from Mum, from Reg, from the house with all its bad memories. It's dark by the time I get back. Mum is already staggering around upstairs. Drunk again. I ignore Reg, make a jam sandwich and go straight to my room. I'm relieved when I wake up next morning. At least Mum left me alone.

* * *

While I know Mum relies on Reg and has come to love him very deeply, I never have or will work out their marriage. How two people with almost nothing in common and from two completely different generations could come together and have an apparently loving union. It may look like a marriage of convenience, but she could never have settled down with a 'normal' man. In Reg she found someone prepared to accept her the way she was and put a roof over her family's heads.

But even if these were the reasons they decided to stay together, their marriage has become much more than that. They almost never go anywhere without each other and they discuss everything together in detail – even though she always gets her own way. I see this more clearly than ever when Reg decides to go on holiday on his own.

Reg has a son called Anthony who lives in Australia. He emigrated many years before and Reg hasn't seen him or his grandkids for the whole of that period. Mum and I have never met him. Contact has been patchy, amounting to birthday and Christmas cards. Mum single-handedly re-ignites their relationship and in some style. She begins by writing to them; they reply with letters and photos of the family. She increases the contact by phone. Although Reg isn't a strong family man, I know this has made him very happy. He is fond of Anthony and has missed him since he emigrated. The contact has grown stronger between Anthony and Reg and both our families. Mum is delighted to do this for Reg. As the contact becomes more regular, the idea of meeting each other comes up but is rejected because of the cost. Anthony can't afford to bring his family back to England and we certainly don't have the money to fly us all over there.

Then Mum has a brainwave. She suggests to Anthony that Reg go to Australia to visit them. Immediately, Anthony says he'll pay half the fare and the idea is set in motion. Mum sets about planning this trip and in 1982, at the age of 72, Reg goes from Halifax, Yorkshire to Perth, Australia. He gets on a coach from Halifax bus station to central London, and transfers himself to Heathrow Airport where he boards a plane for Perth.

Reg has lived all his life in the same village where he was born. He has always worked within a few miles of his home and has never flown before or even left England. He has only been to London once, which was with us in the car. Yet he flies thousands of miles as an old man to spend time with his family whom he hasn't seen for years. This is a big deal for him and for Mum. She is delighted for him, but beside herself with worry, convinced she'll never see him again and doesn't relax until he is safe home.

While Reg is in Australia, they write to each other every day. The letters are written by two people who love each other very much and feel real pain when they are apart. When he returns, Mum is ecstatic beyond belief. But knowing they have this deep, enduring love for each other still only confuses me as to why she hasn't intervened when she knew Reg was beating me. Or at least brought up the topic again for discussion.

Since he's stopped beating me, Reg's involvement has been purely logistical, making sure someone is there when I come home from school. He is entirely indifferent towards me. He doesn't appear to hate me, it's just that he doesn't care. Or so it seems. One incident makes me think he might a little after all.

* * *

I have come home from school one afternoon on the bus and got off at the stop at the bottom of our lane, along with one other boy, Alan Carthy, who lives at the first house up the lane. But as we turn up the lane I see something that makes my heart sink. In front of us are two more boys, Andrew, Reg's grandson from the farm; and one of Andrew's friends.

Andrew has changed since his parents turned against Mum and Reg. I don't know what happened to cause this – all I know is that they don't see much of each other nowadays and I instinctively know that if we do bump into each other something bad will happen. The contact has stopped between Pauline's family and ours and although I occasionally see him walking up and down the lane he usually ignores me. I am already aware that this is a bad situation and I've got used to keeping out of his way, which works most of the time, but as we live up the same road, we have no choice but to walk up together. He and his mate are in front of me and as they walk he says something to his mate and they both laugh and look back at me.

I ignore him and walk more slowly so that they can get further up the lane. Suddenly both of them turn round and walk towards me, blocking my path. It's obvious that Andrew isn't interested in Alan Carthy who skirts round the edge of us and runs off up the lane.

'What do you want, Andrew?' I ask, hardly daring to ask the question.

'Piss off you little bastard,' he swears nastily. 'I'll tell you what I want when I'm good and ready.'

I stand there for what seems like ages with Andrew spitting out abuse at me. I know he is easily capable of hitting me so I just take it without answering back. He keeps coming up close and I can see the hatred in his eyes. I look away and he can tell I'm really scared. That seems to be enough for it not to get physical. He would love me to try fighting him, probably hurting me badly in the process. But he chooses not to hit me. Eventually he decides he's finished with me for the day and walks off up the lane. I'm pretty shaken up and wait until he's out of sight before carrying on walking.

When I get home a few minutes later and tell Reg what has been going on, I don't expect him to say or do anything but what he does do truly surprises me. He drops whatever is in his hand and turns to me, eyes blazing, incandescent with rage.

'Where did this happen?' he says, through gritted teeth.

'Down the road,' I reply, bewildered.

Reg shoots out of the door and down the lane. I can see him from the house and he is moving more quickly than

I've ever seen him move before. Eventually, he returns, completely out of breath and finally calms down.

'The next time that happens, you tell me straight away.'

'Of course, Grandad.'

I'm stunned by all of this. On the surface, it appears that Reg has gone out to defend me against Andrew's bullying, which seems to suggest that he does love me or at least care about me, even though Andrew is his own grandson.

When Mum hears about it, she asks me if I want to learn how to box. I say yes, so we go down to the local community centre in Mystendyke. They don't do boxing lessons but have a karate class. I join up straight away and for several years I go down there every Monday and Wednesday evening for two hours.

It's such a bizarre situation. On the one hand I am learning self-defence so that I can fend off people who want to hurt me. On the other, the one person who has physically and emotionally hurt me for years with his beatings is my stepfather, entrusted to look after me and help bring me up.

Learning karate is a very positive activity for me. It stops me being the whipping boy at school. The bullies will still do the rounds and pick on almost all the boys. But in my relations with the rest of the kids, everything changes.

I have always been easy pickings for any schoolkid to have a go at. It's usually for small things, but I hate it nonetheless. My school clothes are a good starting point. I'm still wearing secondhand clothes that are about as unfashionable as you can get. Most kids in my year wear clothes that bear some relation to the fashion of the day, but from head to toe I have nothing that comes close. Mum has zero interest in fashion whatsoever for herself. She certainly doesn't think I need it either. She believes in function over form at every turn, which even applies to my school bag.

Every boy at school has a sports bag to carry their stuff in, but to my eternal horror and shame, when I started at secondary school Mum bought me a briefcase, a large brown one with separators inside. It was sturdy and strong so it even lasted a long time. After the briefcase had had its day, I was hoping she would eventually listen to my protests and get me a sports bag like all the other boys. But no – she got me something even worse, a traditional brown leather satchel. Even though it has done its job very well and seems to last forever, I'm the only kid in my year to have such a monstrosity. Satchels are associated with girls, which makes me despise it even more.

It's these small differences that make me stand out and become the butt of snide remarks and ridicule. I am still hypersensitive to it, but after learning karate, I can retaliate. In most cases, when kids see I'm not going to take it lying down any more, they leave me be. A few aren't so happy and eventually, after I have a row with one lad over nothing, he demands a fight.

'Fine,' I say. We convene at the usual spot for fights in the school and quite a crowd turn up. It's all about to kick off when someone whispers something in the other lad's ear. I can just about make it out.

'You'd better be careful, John, he does karate,' he said, pointing at me.

Instantly, the other lad's face changes as it dawns on him that a fight with me might not be such a good idea after all. He backs off and that's the end of it. From then on, no-one bothers me, which is fine by me. I don't want to be a fighter, I just want to be left alone. Apart from when it comes to girls, of course.

* * *

I'm more and more aware of girls but even though I am now fast approaching fourteen I have never even kissed a girl, let alone had a proper girlfriend. Girls aren't even slightly interested in me and by now I'm prepared to go out with any girl, irrespective of her looks or what anyone thinks of her.

Then one day my prayers are answered. A girl I vaguely know approaches me.

'Here, David,' she summons.

'Yes,' I reply cautiously, knowing that girls usually enjoy poking fun at me.

'Would you be interested in going out with Sophie?' she enquires.

She asks the question as nonchalantly as if asking whether they have chocolate-flavoured ice cream in the local corner shop. But it's like someone has just plugged me into the National Grid.

I look round, convinced she must have the wrong person.

'Who ... me?' I stutter.

'Yes,' she says, 'meet us over by the steps at lunchtime.'

I can barely contain myself through the following lessons, and at lunchtime I am there like a shot. This is the best news ever. I find myself dreaming about her in class and running like mad in the breaks to spend a few extra seconds with her. I am totally besotted with her, but from the start I can tell she isn't so enamoured with me.

Sophie is slightly overweight, not particularly good looking, with a wide mouth and brown hair. None of the other boys is interested in her but I am, mainly because she's the first girl ever to show interest in me – apart of course from Sally Seymour who dumped me after one date when I was eleven.

Although Sophie has agreed to be my girlfriend, she is obviously not too keen on the physical aspect. We barely kiss or cuddle. Sitting next to her on the steps and putting my arm around her is as good as it gets – not great for a teenage boy with rampant hormones. So I wait patiently, just happy to have a girlfriend.

Then one day during the holidays I go to her house and we end up in her bedroom under some sheets on the floor, and it's there we have our first kiss. I'm not very good at it but that doesn't matter. I have kissed a girl and it feels spectacular. We now have a special connection – and not one like I have with Mum when she's drunk.

I go into school with my head held high. I am no longer the runt of the litter that no-one wants. I am so proud of myself.

This euphoric feeling doesn't last long. Four weeks into the relationship, Sophie ditches me – no reasons, no explanations. I am dropped like a hot cake.

Devastated beyond belief, feeling like my life has come to an end, the sense of desperation and loss crushes me horribly. I am fragile at the best of times and this level of rejection is difficult for me to take. I struggle for some time until it gets too much – and then I do something very silly.

Mum and Reg have gone out one Saturday evening, leaving me alone in the house. I am still thinking about Sophie and can't get her out of my head. I am heartbroken, unable to shake that sinking feeling of loneliness and despair. I have a Sony cassette player which I play constantly. Around this time in 1982 I'm keen on Big Country, Abba, Madness and anything ska – and one song in particular: 'Heartbreaker' by Dionne Warwick.

I sit and play this record over and over again. Each time, it heightens the sadness and the sick feeling in the pit of my stomach I have when I think about Sophie.

Eventually, I can't take it any more. I've had enough. I find some headache tablets in the kitchen and started taking them, one at a time, all the while continuing to play 'Heartbreaker'. The tablets make me feel sick and nauseous, and eventually I start to get really woozy. I decide to stop taking them but by this time I know I'm in a bad way. I don't want Mum to see me like this so I decide the best thing to do is go to bed. Once I lie down and look up, the room starts to spin. I am now very poorly from the tablets but imagine I'll be better in the morning if I can get to sleep. I eventually doze off, thankfully before Mum comes home.

Waking up the next morning, the events of the previous night come flooding back. Immediately, I understand that this has been a lucky escape. I could have died if I had carried on taking the tablets. I become upset again thinking about my ex-girlfriend but this pain of being miserable is quickly replaced with a violent pain in my stomach.

'Mum,' I shout, 'I've got a really bad tummy ache.'

I sob as she comes into my bedroom. She looks into my eyes to see if I really mean it. I have excellent school-attendance records, mainly because she will never let me stay off school unless I'm on the critical list. She won't have any truck with sniffling colds. If I can walk, I go to school. But she can tell this is something different. After all, she is a trained nurse. In any case, there would be no point in my faking it as it's a Sunday, not a school day.

'How bad is it?' she asks.

'Really, really bad. Please get a doctor.'

'Do you think that's necessary?' she questions, knowing this will mean calling a doctor out to the house on a Sunday.

'But Mum, I feel really sick,' I plead. 'Please call a doctor.'

She knows I am a servile child and can see I'm not well. Meanwhile I'm struggling to keep quiet about what has happened the night before, although I want to tell her so she can make me better. Interestingly, she never asks whether this might have been self-inflicted so I never tell her the truth. She calls the doctor and he comes out to the house. He can see no serious symptoms and so goes for the main question.

'What do *you* think caused this then, David?' he asks, like a headmaster talking to a naughty schoolchild.

I know that if I'm going to share what has happened, this is the time to tell him. But I can't get the words out. I'm so used to hiding secrets that this is just one more to add to the list.

'I don't know,' I reply sheepishly.

He looks at me for a few seconds, deciding whether to believe me or not. He must think I'm telling the truth though, as he asks no more questions. He tells Mum to keep me in bed and look after me, and what to do to ease my stomach pains.

Within a few days I'm fine again and realize I've had another lucky escape. I don't want to die – certainly not from an overdose. My fragile personality has been exposed: I have found rejection by Sophie unbearable, to the point of attempting suicide.

I decide to share what has happened with a friend from school. Daniel and I are in the same form and we've become friends. He's a tall, gangly, intelligent, articulate Southerner with a long, thin face and squeaky voice. He is also pro-CND, which is quite unusual in a Northern high school. We are both oddballs and I find myself gravitating towards him. I sometimes go to his house.

Shortly after this incident, Daniel and I are walking in Mystendyke when I blurt it out to him about what I've done. He looks stunned and horrified, and very quickly I realize I've made a big mistake in telling him. He isn't very sympathetic and doesn't want to listen to my problems or fears. He can't understand why I have done it and I realize he could now tell everyone at school. To his credit, he keeps it to himself but he still isn't that interested.

I desperately want to share my pain over Sophie with someone who can help me through it, but Daniel isn't that person. I also thought that if he could understand my half-baked suicide attempt, I might be able to share with him what was going on at home with Mum. But his indifference quickly extinguishes that idea. From now on, I know I have to keep what is happening between Mum and me a secret. No-one must ever find out about it.

* * *

Life at home is slowly getting worse, as Mum's drinking gets more out of control by as each week passes.

There are superficial distractions though. In my second and third year at secondary school I go on a French exchange trip to St Paul in northern France. Students go to France and spend two to three weeks staying in the home of a student their own age; French students then spend the same time at our houses. My French is OK and so is Mum's, which makes this trip the natural choice. It is also cheap: there are no accommodation costs or even flights as we go on the ferry. I would loved to go skiing but that is completely out of the question.

I enjoy every minute of both trips, especially as I stay with the same family. Their house is like a small farm with livestock and miniature horses in a beautiful village with country lanes, a tabac and little new development. My exchange student, Jean-Pierre, is tall and popular. Mum is a brilliant host when he stays. She looks after him really well and, to my relief, abstains from drinking. This is one of the few occasions in recent years that she has remained sober for longer than a few days. Even with her vicious temper, abusive behaviour and selfishness, she still has the ability to be a decent person at the right time when she chooses.

The exchange also gives me more freedom to do things I wouldn't normally be able to do. Until then, I have never drunk at all. Despite Mum's alcoholism, she never lets me drink, not even a sip. Then one evening a party is arranged at the house of one of the English kids. I'm not normally invited to parties, but all the members of the exchange group, including me, are on the invitation list. Bizarrely under the circumstances, the parents have gone out and left the house completely to us. It isn't long before alcohol appears. I haven't brought a bottle with me so it must have come from the parents' supply or what other kids have bought.

I taste some of the drinks and don't like them very much. Spirits are too strong; beer and lager too bitter.

Then I find a drink I like – sherry. The thick sweet liquid becomes my favourite tipple for the night and I keep the bottle totally to myself throughout the evening. Pretty soon, I'm totally drunk and I love it. The carefree, uninhibited feeling is wonderful. I am starting to see why Mum drinks so much. I also love the taste of the sherry, and from now on prefer sweet drinks like cider and liqueurs.

I don't remember much about the evening other than everyone getting drunk and someone threatening suicide. A couple have a big fallout and the girl says she's going to throw herself off the top of a wall at the back of the house. After the kinds of incidents that occur when Mum gets drunk, as far as I am concerned a hysterical girl looking for attention because she's been dumped by her boyfriend doesn't seem excessive. I take it in my stride.

When I get home, Mum cuts me an awful lot of slack because we have Jean-Pierre staying with us and he's in the same state as me. Once he leaves, though, she reverts to her normal ways.

* * *

One of the worst elements of Mum's drinking is her verbal abusiveness. The things she says shock and scare me and I feel she says them just to hurt me and Reg. Sometimes she'll make them up just to get attention. On Sundays we always have a roast meal – Reg usually cooks and Mum sometimes helps.

One Sunday she starts drinking earlier than usual and by the time the meal is ready she is wasted, which means she won't be eating. Reg and I sit and eat our meal while Mum staggers around upstairs. She suddenly comes crashing down the stairs, the door swing open and she stands there, staring at us in the doorway.

'I've got cancer,' she announces. 'I hope you'll all be happy when I'm dead.'

With that she slams the door shut and goes back to bed.

We carry on eating in complete silence. There is nothing we can do and we are never going to get the truth out of her while she is drunk. This isn't excessive behaviour and we've become immune to it to a certain extent, even when she says something as shocking as that.

This level of abusiveness is one reason why she has such a rapid turnover of friends. A new friend will appear on the horizon, become her bosom buddy for a few months and then disappear in a puff of smoke. Although Mum can talk till the cows come how when she wants to, she isn't a good listener. She never understands the concept of being interested instead of interesting and it's difficult to have a flowing conversation with her.

But this doesn't necessarily cause a huge problem compared with the volume and length of her phone calls. Even those fade into insignificance in comparison with what happens once alcohol is involved. Whatever problems people have with her on the phone became amplified a thousand times when she's drunk. Sometimes the drunken conversations may be funny or easy to pass off. Sometimes she phones before she is completely smashed and the conversations are fairly normal. But pretty soon she'll be phoning up and saying things that are personal and abusive. It only takes a few such calls before the other person terminates their friendship.

One night, she decides to phone Dad in the States. He doesn't answer so she leaves a message – which lasts an incredible 45 minutes. To speak non-stop for 45 minutes is a skill in itself but to do it to an answering machine on a transatlantic call to a man from whom you've been divorced for many years is almost beyond comprehension. This is before the time of cheap telecommunications and it costs her a fortune. Her phone bills must be horrendous. At some level she must know what she's doing when she is drunk when she receives the bills and sees the calls she has been making, but it doesn't stop her, not even when she factors in the personal cost. Her telephone problems isolate friends and family alike.

In the years to come, even Anthony, Reg's son in Australia, will do the same because of Mum's abuse of them through drinking. This, despite the fact that she has carefully orchestrated the once-in-a-lifetime trip to Australia for Reg.

Reg's split from his family up the lane is now absolute. This has been demonstrated in very dark circumstances. Michael, Reg's grandson, always rode his bike at high speed in the narrow lanes around our house. If I was out walking the dogs and heard him coming I'd pick them up. I didn't like him or trust him not to hit the dogs out of sheer spite. He had previously been nasty to Mum, calling her 'Bitch!' when I was out with her picking blackberries in the field one day. It shook me up but unusually she had been very calm about it, carrying on picking the fruit while receiving the abuse.

One night Michael rode his bike into a wall at high speed and was killed. No-one came from the farm to tell Reg what had happened or to invite him to the funeral. Reg is a strong man mentally and never lets on how he feels, but it must hurt him nonetheless. Of course it's all related to Mum's drinking.

And still it doesn't stop her. Her drinking actually increases which only makes things worse. But I can't change my telephone number or terminate our relationship like family and friends. I have to put up with it.

I am now fourteen. I am growing into an adult, sexually aware of myself and my body. I guess she notices this too because there is a decisive change in her. When drunk, she'll still come to my room, creating mayhem with the light and blankets as she always did and she still lies on my bed. But now her demands are different and I'll never forget the night they change …

* * *

She comes into my room, blind drunk, her eyes completely glazed over. She has to stand leaning against the door frame as she can't stand at all without support. She lurches over to my bed, grabbing it to steady herself. I've heard her coming so I'm out of my bed, standing to one side.

She lies on the bed, spreads her legs and turns her head on one side to find out where I am. With the combination of being drunk and me being in the corner, she can't see me.

'David,' she murmurs.

I ignore her.

'David!' she says a little louder.

I still ignore her.

'David!' she shouts.

'Yes, Mum!' I reply.

My heart sinks. I don't have it in me to carry on ignoring her, so I prepare myself to receive her usual demands. But this time it isn't coming. This time, she has a different demand.

'Come over here and fuck me, David.'

Shockwaves run through my body. I stand there absolutely stupefied, unable to believe what I'm hearing. After all these years and everything that has happened, she has sunk to a new level. I'm frozen to the spot, unable to move, trying to compute what my mother has asked of me.

'Come over here and fuck me now, David!' she repeats in a more commanding voice.

I look at my mother, lying on my bed. She is gently writhing from side to side, murmuring rubbish and repeating that she wants me to have sex with her. The repetition of her demand would normally have been enough for me to do as I was told. But this time, I know I have to fight back and say no. I walk out of the room, down the stairs and sit in the dining room, head in my hands, completely shell-shocked, unable to comprehend what she has just said.

She staggers downstairs after me. As she enters the dining room, she stares at me with disdain and without saying anything goes into the kitchen and begins cooking some food. I stay with her and watch her to make sure she doesn't come to any harm. Even though it's some time before she goes to bed, it feels like a few minutes.

The time goes in a blur as I am desperately trying to come to terms with the fact that my own mother now wants to have sex with me. Even though I am a teenager with raging hormones, the mere thought of having sex with her disgusts me. It makes me feel sick in a way I've never felt before.

I have to find a way out of all this. Something has to change. I'm on the edge and I don't know how much longer I can stand it.

9

Night-Runner

I have begun to find a way out – or at least a way that's different from how I've dealt with things in the past.

I have decided to look after my body. I am going to get fit.

And to begin with, karate is the key.

I pass my grades every three months, and continue doing so until I am 18, five years in total. I enjoy the discipline and the fact that I have stuck at it when most people drop out. Another sport I become interested in is distance running. I decide one summer that I am going to improve my running ability. I am never a sprinter as I don't have the necessary explosive power. But I do have stamina and can carry on running way past the point where most of the other kids have dropped out.

I train myself by going out running at home. I have no idea what I am doing so I just have a go anyway. I design a circular cross-country course, starting on the flat, going up through some woodland and then a steep hill. It finishes off with running along the road and crossing some fields. I time myself, looking to beat my personal best every time I go out running. I love the feeling of challenging myself, the fact that it is hard work. The harder it is, the greater the rewards seem to be.

I work at it all summer, driving myself on to improve my times and designing ever tougher training courses. But I have no idea if I am any good or not. I am running courses where I have no benchmark to measure myself against. I will only know once I get back to school after the summer break. As usual, I tell no-one what I'm doing and just keep it to myself. The proof will be the first time we go out for a cross-country run in the PE lesson.

To my joy and satisfaction, all the work in the holidays has paid off. Instead of lounging around in the middle of the group, I'm out at the front, challenging for top position. This motivates me to push myself even harder. I spend the whole winter going out as many nights as I can. Pretty soon I'm winning at school.

Then comes the big race.

Every year there is a house cross-country race, a prestigious event with certificates awarded. In my fourth year, I come second; in the fifth year I win. It is easily the best thing I have achieved in five years at that school. I will always remember being called out to get my certificate at assembly in front of the whole school and the clapping ringing in my ears.

I am now learning more about myself. I find success electrifying. I love it. It is like a drug to me. I like the attention coming my way. Even better than that, attention for the right reasons. At school, boys are respected who can do well at sport. I am no good at rugby, football, cricket or basketball but being one of the top runners in my year is good enough for me to earn the respect I crave and now deserve.

I always knew I had a competitive streak, but have often suppressed it. I enter an orienteering competition on behalf of the Scout group and win, and again I love the feeling of winning. It is the first competition the Scout group has won in a long time and I feel very proud. But I know I'm not a team player. I have friends at school but I'm happy to be alone as well. That's why I enjoy karate and running. I like the solitude of running, and karate is essentially an individual pursuit. They are perfect for me, things I can do alone while gaining the admiration of others.

Unfortunately, Mum isn't one of them. She never shows any interest at all, which upsets me a great deal. Despite what is happening between us, I still look to her for support, encouragement and guidance. None is forthcoming in relation to my sports. But even though winning at school is amazing, my running also has peripheral benefits.

I'm soon going out running in the middle of the night.

* * *

Unfortunately getting a girlfriend isn't one of those peripheral benefits. Even with my new-found status as one of the top runners in my year, girls are still not particularly interested in me. So I look elsewhere and soon find a wellspring for a succession of girlfriends.

My school is near a town called Ludden Bridge, lying in a valley running from Ludden in Yorkshire through to Blackholme (Black for short) in Lancashire. There has always been huge rivalry between the two counties since Yorkshire lost the War of the Roses nearly 400 years ago.

It's a platitude that people from Yorkshire and Lancashire don't get on. But as a young lad, this antagonism definitely extends to the lads that live in each town.

There are organized groups of lads from Ludden Bridge and Blackholme who actively go looking for trouble in each others' town and patrol their own area. Both groups are highly territorial and don't like it if anyone from either place comes onto their patch. I'm not part of that group but I still know it isn't a good idea to go to Blackholme unless you fancy getting into trouble. But this doesn't bother me. In fact, I find it quite thrilling. I am slowly morphing from being a lad who wants to blend into the background into one who isn't that bothered about his welfare and fancies a bit of danger. Going to Blackholme seemed an exciting adventure.

One Friday night, I get my chance. A lad in my year lives in Blackholme. I still have no idea why he travels six miles to my school when Blackholme has its own second-ary school only a mile from his home. He has a house party and I'm invited along with some other lads. I jump at the chance, although I know what it means. If the local lads know we're at the party we can potentially be in big trouble. Stories are rife about lads that have been hurt before, but a few boys are going up together and so we feel safety in numbers. Of course, I don't tell Mum about the potential danger, otherwise she would never let me go.

The party is good and I meet a girl. Val is slim and attractive, with shoulder-length hair and she flirts with me. I can't believe my luck that she wants to go out with me. I think it's only because I am from a different place but I don't care. I go home floating on air.

As she lives in Blackholme, I have to travel down that end of the valley to see her and she comes to see me at Ludden Vale.

Mum's surprisingly cool – in a good way – about Val spending time with me in my bedroom. One evening when we come downstairs straight after some serious snogging and heavy petting, she stops us in the hall.

'By the way,' she says to me calmly, 'I think your jumper must be back to front.'

One night we go to a junior disco at the Winter Ballroom in Blackholme. There are three of us who travel from down the valley. Word has got around we're there and very quickly a group of lads turn up outside. As they don't want to pay, only the biggest one pays and comes inside – a good-looking lad in suit, shirt and tie.

He looks around, spots me, then walks straight up to me on the dance floor.

'What the fuck are you doing here – and with this slag?' he asks, nodding at Val.

Without replying, I hit him straight in the face as hard as I could. He goes down on the floor. Knowing how to punch from karate means he isn't going to come back for more. He picks himself up and walks back towards the door.

'You're fucking dead,' he shouts as he leaves the room.

I look at Val. Her face is ashen.

'You do realize that's Ron Masterton?' she says with a quiver in her voice. 'There's going to be trouble now.'

'Come on, we'd better go,' I say.

Joe, a friend from school who lives in Blackholme, runs over. He's a friendly lad, overweight but good-humoured, with a bunch of friends, and I tag along when he has the party.

'Bloody hell, Dave, you've started something now. You'll have to go out of the back door and go to my house.'

Along with my mates and their girlfriends, I leave by the back door and down a side street. As we cross a main road, I can see a bunch of lads gathering. One of them clocks me and shouts, 'Oi! He's down here!'

We run as fast as we can back to Joe's house while the others are still chasing us. When we get there, everyone looks worried and nervous, but I think it's the most exciting thing in the world. By this time I love fighting and the thrill of the chase. I have also developed an inbuilt kamikaze attitude where I'm not even bothered if I get caught and get a beating. But as it turns out I never see Ron Masterton again.

* * *

I'm turning into an adrenaline junkie. It isn't enough to be going to Blackholme where I can potentially get hurt. I want to take it to the edge where the Wolves (the Blackholme lads) know I'm there and will come and find me.

Val and I only last four weeks before she dumps me for someone else. We haven't even had sex as I'm still a virgin and rather shy. But I know who her new boyfriend is and am sure she's been seeing him while seeing me. So I go up to Blackholme on my own, walking round the streets looking for him. When I see him on his pushbike, I step out into the middle of the road, punch him straight off the bike, drag him onto the pavement and punch him three or four times in the face. I shout at him and he quivers. I don't even tell him to stop seeing Val, I just want to punch his lights out. It won't make any difference anyway. They carry on going out together and I move on.

I meet Suzy at a youth club while still seeing Val. She makes a pass at me, which I'm not used to, and I soon realize she's more sexually aware than most of the girls I've known. Within a few days of meeting, we go to a party and have sex on the bedroom floor of someone's house. It's the first time I've had sex and I don't care that it's on the floor and not somewhere more romantic.

Suzy really likes me; she's a friendly girl, shorter than average and a little tomboyish-looking, with short brown hair and she tends to wear jeans rather than skirts. She's a little reckless like me, and I'm still going up to Blackholme on a regular basis, which is also exciting as I never know when I'm going to come across the local lads. I do not go looking for it but I'm always up for a ruck if it comes my way and will never back down, although this can go against me as I am usually on my own.

While going to Suzy's on the bus one day I see three lads from Blackholme at the side of the road. I shout some abuse at them out of the window and hold up two fingers in a V sign. They don't take it well, shouting abuse back at me.

A few weeks later I'm on the bus and the same three lads get on. They spot me and say nothing. I pretend I don't know them and get up for my stop. As I walk down the stairs, all three jump on me and give me a kicking, but I manage to get one of them and punch him hard in the face.

I stagger off the bus with a bruised face, absolutely furious. I stand at the side of the road, shouting at them on the bus, 'You fucking wankers! I'll take any of you on one to one. Get off that bus now, you soft Blackholme bastards.'

People walking along the street stare at me in disgust.

'What are you looking at, you old cow?' I sneer.

I know that this is totally uncharacteristic of the way the old David would have behaved – the weedy, submissive and compliant little ginger-haired schoolboy who wouldn't say boo to a goose – but I've had enough of that David. Where did being submissive and compliant ever get me? It's time I stood up for myself, and taught them all who they were dealing with.

I go up to Suzy's and she sorts me out. I'm all for going out to find them to get my own back but she manages to convince me that this is a bad idea.

I enjoy being this new David. It feels dangerous and slightly out of control. After one party I go to with some other lads from down the same end of the valley as me, I get involved in a chase. I'm carrying an empty vodka bottle and I smash it, ready to use the jagged edge if we get caught. I'm sure I would do if I were cornered.

Despite everything that has gone on at home, despite all the beatings and thrashings that Reg has given me down the years, which Mum knew about all along, she has never encouraged me to be violent and she has never knowingly been physically violent towards me. I have learned karate but she wouldn't be happy if she knew I was into fighting. She used to physically discipline me when I was a young child but she never does anything like that now. With Mum, it's more psychological. If I do something wrong, she'll scream and shout, going on about it for days. It's always easier to do as I'm told than have the aggravation. I may like the rush of a potential chase and fight, but at home I want a peaceful life.

By now I have become adept at dealing with her when she's drunk and can read the situation like a book …

* * *

*I know what she's going to do and how she's going to do it. Once
I hear her outside my room I already have one foot out of bed. If
she comes through the door I'm off the bed like a jackrabbit. If
she wants sex with me she'll lie down on the bed.*

'Fuck me, David, pleeeease,' she pleads.

*Hearing this tears my mind apart and so once she lies down
on the bed I'm off out the door as quickly as I can. I don't want
to hear it.*

*But sometimes I doze off and she catches me half asleep. If she
gets to me before I climb out of bed, she'll try to play with my
penis. Despite my greatest efforts, this can give me a semi-
erection. Usually she's too drunk to notice this but if she does, it
excites her and she wants more.*

*I'm disgusted with myself at my involuntary response. In fact,
the whole situation makes me feel sick. It's the conflict between
her asking me to do something and my having to say no. Despite
being fifteen and knowing how wrong this is, asking to have sex
is a very powerful request from a mother to a son. My natural
reaction at all times is to do what my mother tells me. But when
she demands sex, I resist completely. She tries various different
ways of coaxing and pressurizing me. One method is emotional
blackmail.*

'You'd do it if you loved me.'

On other occasions she's more abrupt or abusive.

'Do as your mother tells you to.'

'You just don't care about me.'

'You're such a selfish bastard.'

*The emotional pressure and manipulation are intense and
unbearable. The easiest way is not to be there when she speaks the
words to me. So I do everything in my power to stay awake*

when she's been drinking. But sometimes I do fall asleep through sheer exhaustion or because I am naturally tired.

She doesn't know this when she comes to my room. But once she sees it, she's fully prepared to take maximum advantage. She turns on the light and enters my room. Before I have even reacted she pulls back my blankets and jumps on top of me.

I wake up to find my mother straddling me, trying to insert my penis into her vagina.

'Mum,' I say, still half asleep, 'get off me.'

She ignores me completely and continues trying to have sex with me. I'm still not fully awake, and as an automatic reaction, violently push her away. She falls and bangs her head very hard on the floor, then gets up looking even more dazed than usual and goes downstairs.

* * *

At this moment I have no doubt that if she could rape me she would. Because of this I feel grateful for one thing – that I'm a boy with an alcoholic mother. If I were a girl with an alcoholic father who has been as sexually aggressive as my mother, then my situation would be far worse. But if I didn't ignore her requests I would end up having a full sexual relationship with my own mother. At one point I have even considered it, wondering if having sex with her could pacify her and make her happy. Whenever she's asked me to play with her vagina, it's made her quiet and once she's had enough she leaves me alone. I have felt uncomfortable doing this but do it anyway because she tells me to. Maybe the same could happen now.

But the difference is that I'm much older. I know what we did when I was young was very wrong but this is different now. It is completely off the chart. Plus I have a choice. I could never live with myself if I were to do it, no matter what pressure came from her. In the mornings after the nights before, Mum wouldn't have to deal with what happened because she wouldn't remember it. I would remember and would have to deal with a whole new level of pain for the rest of my life.

The second problem is that I have no-one to confide in. I have some friends but no-one really close. I have already told a friend about my attempted suicide, which proved to be a bad mistake and I'm not going to do the same thing again. Suzy and I get on very well but I don't feel I can tell her anything like this. Reg is too old and doesn't care about me, and in any case the idea of telling him what has been going on between me and Mum is, as usual, unthinkable. And of course, I can't talk to Mum about it when she's sober because she doesn't even know what she's doing when she's drunk.

I've learned to keep things to myself and I cope with it on my own. And the way I choose to cope with it at this stage in my adolescence is by deciding to become a criminal mastermind.

* * *

I'm not sure what has driven me to it but one thing that may have been a trigger is that I have recently developed a taste for expensive sports clothes. This is very strange as Mum has always been proud of the fact that she can find clothes that cost next to nothing. My interest in good clothes certainly doesn't come through her. But the main issue is that as I don't have money to pay for them, I will steal it.

Ironically, it's Mum's drinking that allows me to do this. She's a lifelong insomniac, always having a ready supply of sleeping pills to get her through the night. On nights when she isn't drinking, she often gets up and makes a cup of tea. She has a bedside light and reads until she falls asleep again. But when she's been drinking, her sleep follows a different pattern altogether. Once she goes to sleep, the drink ensures that she sleeps heavily and won't wake up for anything until morning. She doesn't even get up to use the toilet – a rubber sheet on her bed being evidence that she wets the bed on drinking nights.

So Mum and Reg are fast asleep; I am wide awake. I have been chasing around the house after her and have had to stay awake for some time after she's gone to sleep, just in case she wakes up again. This presents the perfect combination. Being wide awake, coupled with Mum's deep sleep, means that the best time to commit burglaries is the middle of the night. Once I'm sure she's fast asleep, I get dressed – usually a pair of shorts and sweat shirt. I'm running every night at home and am extremely fit. It makes sense for me to run to my intended burglary destination.

I commit my first burglary at an obvious place – my own school. Despite assuming it will be completely alarmed, I go anyway. The school is only a couple of miles from where I live but the great thing is that I can run over the tops of the hills to get there and keep away from any police patrolling the main road. Living in the Pennines, you go out of your house and the land goes either up or down. I am running faster than I have ever run before and the adrenaline rush is amazing.

Once at the school, I sneak into the main courtyard, my heart almost jumping out of my chest. I am excited, nervous, loving every minute of it. I try all the doors and they're locked. I look for open windows and there aren't any. Realizing I'm going to have to smash a window, I pick up a stone and throw it. The noise is deafening. I run out of the courtyard and hide behind some bushes on the main drive. I can't hear an alarm but I want to see if someone has heard the window smash.

I wait patiently until figuring it's OK to go back. Even though breaking the window has seemed reckless, I'm more careful with everything else. I take great pains to remove all the broken pieces of glass, including any rough edges in case anyone turns up and I need to get back out of the window quickly.

The school is dark, empty, surreal: instead of 1200 kids there's just one – me. I try the office. The window is locked but I carefully prise it open. Inside I find a tin with some petty cash. I steal that, then get out of the window and run back home as fast as I can. I let myself back into the house quietly, get undressed and back into bed.

It's nearly 3 am but I can't sleep. My heart is beating like crazy, I'm so excited. I have committed my first burglary and it feels fantastic. I have achieved my goal of stealing money and can buy the clothes I yearn for. I don't sleep another wink all night but still get up in the morning with a spring in my step.

Going back to school in the morning is a strange feeling, especially seeing the boarded-up window which I've broken just a few hours earlier. It's cool knowing that I know how that happened and who's done it and that not another person in the world knows apart from me.

I have learned how to keep *bad* secrets from everyone else, like the secrets of my mother's drinking and the nature of our relationship. But to me this is a *good* secret and I enjoy knowing something is just for me. The moral implications of what I have done never enter my head. On the contrary, I am delighted that I've found something I am really good at. I have planned and executed a successful burglary and for that I should be congratulated and pleased with myself.

* * *

This foray into petty crime spurs me on to more, with varying success. Next I attempt to break into my local junior school which I have attended between the ages of six and eleven. I take the same line as before, going round the back of the building and throwing a brick through a window. Unfortunately, the school is alarmed and it goes off the moment the brick smashes the glass. I immediately turn tail and run home. Back in bed, I lie there, bitterly disappointed. It isn't a good feeling to come back with nothing.

10

Loose Cannon

Up until now, I've had mixed success with my burglaries and haven't really made much money out of them. I need to burgle somewhere that something of value. Then, one morning in the paper shop, I have a brainwave: I decide to rob it. Mum and Reg's joint income is low and I only receive a small amount of spending money each week. If I want any more, I have to earn it myself. So from the earliest age possible, I've had a morning paper round.

I have to get up at six, run down to the paper shop, deliver my papers and be home by 7.30. I like doing it and the money I earn from it. But the shop I work from is to provide me with much more than some extra spending cash. It is to be the location of my next burglary. I think that there must be some cash lying around and the cigarettes alone will be worth a fortune at school with the number of smokers I can sell to.

I am excited with my idea and set about planning every single aspect down to the last detail. I need to do the robbery in the middle of the night. This isn't a problem as my sleep pattern is shot to pieces because of Mum, and I'm used to getting by on little sleep. I need to learn more about the shop and the police patrols. I have nearly been rumbled before by the police and consider myself lucky to have got away. This time nothing will be left to chance.

I spend two nights staking out the shop between two and four in the morning, sitting on partially hidden stone steps opposite the shop. I note the traffic and any movement in the shop. Most importantly, I note down when the police come past. I am proud of myself for being so thorough and am convinced I'm not going to get caught with such excellent preparation. Getting caught is for fools who are not intelligent enough to think a plan through. I am brighter than that.

I wait until Mum has gone to sleep after a drinking session, dress myself in black and go down to the shop, taking a large holdall with me to carry the tobacco and money. I wait in the shadows for traffic to come along to muffle the sound of breaking glass. Smashing a window would create a lot of noise. Even though the shop is on a row of other businesses, there are residential houses nearby. I don't want to wake anyone.

I am patient. I know it has to be the right kind of vehicle. Eventually, a noisy truck comes along. I wait in a spot where the driver can't see me. As he passes, I gently smash one corner of a window pane in the front of the shop, then quickly run across the road to my previous hiding place on the stone steps and wait. I want to be sure no-one has heard anything and that the police are not on their way.

After an eternity, I creep back across the road and carefully remove the glass. Soon I have cleared a hole big enough for me to get through and ease myself into the shop. In the drawers I find £100 cash and some Saverstrips – pre-paid discounted bus tickets and just as valuable because Mum gives me money to buy them. Now I can pocket the cash and she will be none the wiser. I fill the bag with tobacco. By selling it at school I'll make more money from this one burglary than I've earned in a year doing my paper round.

One nervous moment is when a police car goes past the shop. I have ascertained they won't be patrolling while I'm in the shop. I hide behind the counter but thankfully, on this occasion it isn't necessary. They have their blue lights on and are speeding to an emergency, going way too fast to notice a small smashed pane of glass in a shop window.

Once the bag is full, I carefully climb out the same way I entered. The paper shop is near the canal so I decide to dump my bag there. I place it in some bushes, out of view from anyone who might be walking their dog in the morning. It is 4 am when I arrive home. I am floating. This is about as exciting as life can get. I feel wonderful and am loving every minute of it. I have planned and executed a robbery which has gone like clockwork. I feel so proud of myself.

I really don't feel like getting up to do my paper round but if I don't turn up the morning after a burglary, it might look suspicious. I also have to do it earlier than normal if I am going to have enough time to pick up the bag and take it to school. Without having slept, I get up at 5.30 and go down to the paper shop I have broken into a few hours ago. I look at the boarded-up window and pile of glass, still unable to believe I have done that. My heart is in my mouth when I walk through the door. I can barely speak.

'What's happened there, Ian?' I say.

He is marking the papers. 'Some bastard's broken in and nicked a load of stuff.' He glances up. 'Anyway, how come you're in early?'

'Can't sleep,' I reply, not wanting to look him in the eye and sure he'll see my guilt if he does.

'Well, your bag's not quite ready. Give me a minute.'

I stand there while he finishes off my bag. Now I am feeling uncomfortable. Breaking in during the night is one thing, but being at the scene of the crime a few hours later is making me queasy.

He does my bag and I do my round in record time. I shoot off, running to get home as quickly as possible. I have breakfast and make some noise about wanting to go to school early. Mum has a hangover so she doesn't question me. I go to the canal bank, pick up the bag from the bushes and set off for school.

As soon as I arrive I approach one lad who I know is a smoker, asking him if he wants some cheap tobacco. When I open the bag and he sees how much I have, his face lights up. He looks like Christmas has come early. By morning break, every smoker in the school knows about my bag. I am doing a roaring trade.

For the first time ever I am really popular. I have never had so many people interested in me. I know it is only for the cheap tobacco but it feels fantastic. By lunchtime, students are scouring the school to find me and my stash. I start afternoon classes on a tremendous high. I can't concentrate as I envisage a life of crime where I will commit one burglary after another and sell the proceeds. I don't need exams and qualifications any more and can even see a way of getting away from Mum. It seems the perfect solution to let me start a new life.

Then it all changes in an instant.

As I am gazing out of the window in the first lesson after dinner, someone comes to my classroom and whispers something to the teacher. He looks straight at me and says the last words I want to hear.

'David, go to the Headmaster's office.'

I freeze. Every student in class turns and looks at me. By now, they know I'm the guy with the tobacco but they don't know where it has come from. They've probably guessed that this visit to the Head is something to do with that. I get up from my seat and go to the Head's office. It may not be so bad. There is no way they could have known I was the one who'd committed the burglary and they couldn't have linked the tobacco in the school with what was stolen from the shop. Besides, if it were really that serious the Head would have come and got me himself.

I don't feel overly concerned as I walk the empty corridors. Mr Raymond, the Head, is a real pussycat, a tall, grey-haired man with a plummy voice at odds with our Northern working-class school. I'll lie and deny everything if asked and surely it will go no further.

I knock on his office door.

'Come in.'

Now there is a problem. The voice on the other side of the door isn't the Headmaster's. It is Mr Price, the Deputy Head. He is a different proposition altogether. He has a fierce reputation and has suspended boys for things that have previously gone unpunished.

I open the door gingerly, not really wanting to go in. There are two chairs facing each other in the middle of the room, without a desk or table between them.

'Shut the door and sit down, David,' he says.

We sit down. Without pausing for breath, he leans forward and comes out with it. 'I know about the burglary this morning in your paper shop,' he says calmly.

Holy shit! My head immediately starts to spin. This isn't part of the plan. How the hell does he know? I don't know what to do. I look around as if for some intervention to pull me out of this mess.

'I've spoken to the police and they want to speak to you about it,' Mr Price continues.

It is clear from what he's saying that he not only knows about the robbery but has enough evidence to link me to it. I have been selling a ton of cigarettes only a few hours after a robbery has been reported from a shop where I have been working. The coincidence is just too great and I must have been mad thinking I could get away with it. By now, I am hyperventilating, trying to grasp the magnitude of the problem. I look up at Mr Price and for a second contemplate confessing everything to him there and then.

The contemplation passes very quickly. I am feeling distinctly claustrophobic and know I have to get out of the office. I push my chair back hard, bolting for the door. Mr Price is a fat old guy and there's no way he's going to try and chase me. If he'd got hold of me I would have definitely hit him to get away. As I go out of the door there is another girl waiting in the corridor whom I know.

'See you later,' I gasp, hardly able to get the words out.

I run off down the corridor. It is class time so the school is completely empty, devoid of anyone who might impede my progress. I am fit and quick and out of the school gates in a matter of seconds. I look back anxiously to see if anyone is chasing me. There's nobody following. I slow to a walking pace, keeping an eye out for the police who must surely be on their way. My heart is jumping out of my chest and I can't breathe properly.

I need to take stock of a situation that is now completely out of control. I begin to think about the consequences of my actions. The police are now involved and I have no idea what could happen with them. But that doesn't worry me the most: Mum will find out what I have done. She will be devastated. She is a highly strung woman and I know my actions will cause her untold emotional damage and I want to protect her from that. This, despite the terrible things she does to me when drunk and despite the way I myself have recently caused my life to catapult out of control.

As ridiculous as it may seem, I start thinking of ways in which she may not need to be told. I soon reach the roadside where I catch my bus home sometimes. I stand there, becoming increasingly agitated.

A dinner lady who has just finished her shift comes down and stands at the bus stop near me. She looks at me quizzically as I am obviously supposed to be in school. We don't speak.

As time goes on I become increasingly desperate. I don't want to face the police or Mum's disapproval. I can't think clearly and don't know what to do. I want the decision to be taken away from me and think it will. After doing a runner from the Head's office, I assume that something will happen. Maybe a teacher will follow me down to the road and march me back to the Headmaster's office. Or the school will phone the police and a car will take me to the station.

But nothing happens, nothing at all.

Standing there contemplating my future, I am dreading what might happen. The police could prosecute me; I'll get a criminal record; my home life will get even worse. Mum is hugely susceptible to stress and will go mad when she finds out. Then she'll drink more and visit me more times in my bedroom. I feel similar to how I felt when I was dumped by my first girlfriend and took an overdose – as if life is going to be so bad in the future that I may as well end it now. I turn and say something to the dinner lady – I don't even know what, but it freaks her out and she starts to panic.

Then I do it. I walk out in front of a car. It swerves and misses me but I'm not to be deterred. I walk towards a second car coming down the road, determined to get hit by the vehicle. That swerves and misses me too. I carry on walking down the road into oncoming traffic. Eventually a third car hits me straight on.

* * *

The next thing I remember is waking up in hospital. I haven't broken a single bone. The car was being driven by a Catholic priest.

Mum is sitting on a chair beside me. She looks like the weight of the world is on her shoulders as I knew she would. She's nearly lost her son and isn't taking it well. She has also just discovered I have become a juvenile criminal and the police will be involved. The only thing I can never understand is how they have made the connection. But once they do, there is no doubt they've twigged that it was me.

This isn't her happiest hour as a mother, nor mine as a son.

'How are you feeling, David?' she asks with tears in her eyes.

'I feel fine, Mum,' grasping her hand.

'What happened at the paper shop?'

'I don't know, Mum, I can't remember a thing,' I lie earnestly.

Despite my dire position and just having woken up after having been in a car accident, I have already devised a plan – to say that I've lost my memory and can't remember a thing – but she's always able to read me like a book and she immediately cottons on to me.

'Come on, now, David, tell the truth,' she gently coaxes.

I confess all. She listens in silence, horrified, especially that I'd been going out in the middle of the night. She passed no comment or judgement and looked shattered.

The police arrive shortly after and I tell them the whole story too. Considering everything, they deal with me in a pretty sympathetic manner. Even though I am in a dreadful situation they do say one thing that perks me up no end. They were surprised when they discovered it was a schoolboy who'd committed the crime. By the way the robbery had been meticulously and carefully executed they had assumed it had been a professional burglar.

Unfortunately, this fills me with an overwhelming sense of pride.

When I get home, the Deputy Head, Mr Price, comes to see me. He is always known as a real ogre at school but he is genuinely concerned. When I go back to school most of the students keep their distance. Previously I have got on OK with most students but I'm already quite a loner and this incident only accentuates this. Most kids would have been inquisitive, wanting to know what happened. But with me, they become wary of the weird kid who has robbed a shop and tried to commit suicide. They probably now see me as a loose cannon and have decided it's better to stay away.

Some take the opposite approach though. A couple of students to whom I've never spoken before say that if I want to talk anything through I can go to them. Because of them and others I come to understand that my 'suicide' attempt has had a bigger impact on other people than me.

Years later I discover that Mum wrote to Dad in early 1983 after this incident, describing it as a suicide attempt. In his reply Dad wrote, 'I never imagined for one moment that he might be suicidal.' So the police, school, students, Mum, even Dad, have all taken it a lot more seriously than I have. I don't think I genuinely want to die at this point, just as I hadn't wanted to die when I had previously taken an overdose.

But there is one difference this time. When I wanted to stop taking the tablets, I did just that and put myself to bed. I woke up in the morning because I had chosen to live. The problem with being hit by a car is that I have no choice about the outcome. When I later talk about it with Mum she explains that I have been a lot closer to a potentially fatal injury than I had realized.

I know nothing about the law and so I don't know what will happen next with the police.

Mum has given them a great impression that I come from a very good home. Of course, to her and others looking on, I do.

By the time we end up at the police station, the police have decided to give me a second chance. The police inspector takes me into his office and gives me a proper dressing down. I have never been a mouthy child and look suitably sorry for myself. I apologize profusely, saying I'll never do it again.

In the end, for planning and carrying out a well-thought-through burglary in the middle of the night and stealing hundreds of pounds of stock and cash that I have then tried to sell at my school, I am just given a police caution.

It's the worst thing the police could have done.

* * *

The caution has zero effect on me. In fact, the only thing I'm sorry about it that I've been caught.

Almost as soon as I leave the police station, I decide to commit more burglaries. It makes me feel great and I figure I'm good at it. The police have effectively told me I am operating at the same level as professional burglars. My only problem has been offloading the stolen goods. I just need to do that bit differently. So I now view myself as a successful burglar as I have never having been actually caught in the act of doing it.

Partly through mental anxiety, partly because I want to, I decide to commit another burglary. I have faithfully promised Mum and the police it won't happen again, but I've lied through my teeth to them both.

I decide to be more adventurous for my next job.

I want the money to buy fashionable clothes. The best jumpers you can buy at this time are Pringle jumpers and I want one so badly it hurts. The place to get a Pringle jumper is a shop in Halifax. I know it well from trips to town when, like any kid, I have my nose pressed up against the window looking at all the things I can't afford. I know the shop has a huge front window so I figure all I need to do is smash the window and steal whatever's in the window. There has to be something that I can either wear or sell.

I take a small crowbar from the garage. Reg has a ton of rusting tools all over the place that he never uses and he'll never miss a small crowbar. I wait until Mum has a drinking binge. When the night comes, I watch over her as usual until I know she's fast asleep. Then I get changed. I put on a pair of running trainers, shorts and a red sweatshirt that says 'Paris' with a picture of the Eiffel Tower. I bought it last year on my second French exchange. It's now in tatters, but I still love it.

The shop I'm going to break into is four miles away. The only downside is I have to run on the main road down the valley. Going over the tops is too much of a deviation and will take too long. As this is the only main road, there's an increased chance of the police using it; I can safely assume that a 15-year-old running in shorts and carrying a crowbar will automatically get stopped. So I devise a simple plan. The moment I hear a car coming up behind me, I will jump into a bus shelter or hide behind a wall, waiting until the car has passed and will then carry on running.

I set off for Halifax at a brisk pace. Running this distance isn't a problem, neither is carrying a small crowbar. I am motivated and want to come back with something. The adrenaline is pumping, giving me extra energy. I love this. I feel alive and like the fact that it's the middle of the night. I'm become nocturnal, preferring to walk late at night when it's quiet and still. I settle into a rhythm but as each car comes up behind me I have to stop, find a hiding spot and stand in the shadows while it goes past. I get cheesed off with doing this so I try glancing over my shoulders when I hear a car. I've decided that if I see one with a blue light on top, I'll dart into the shadows. A few cars pass and this seems to work. Then all hell breaks loose.

A car comes up behind me and I turn my head. I can't see it properly and before I know where I am, it has pulled up next to me. It's a police car. The officer in the passenger seat has his window down. He can see the crowbar and speaks to me through the window, opening the car door at the same time.

'What's going on here then, son?'

It seems patronizing but it's obviously a valid question. I'm a strange sight to see in the middle of the night. The moment I see and hear him, I drop the crowbar and turn tail, running back the way I've come. He's now out of the police car, running after me. But there's no way he's going to catch me. I'm off like a bullet.

'Catch him!' he shouts to his partner.

The driver of the police car starts reversing the car with blue lights flashing and siren on. I can hear the corner of the open door scraping on the ground. He's catching up with me so I jump over a wall and run into a small wooded area and across a smaller road at the other side. I relax, trying to get my breath back.

But now I can see the illumination of the police car's blue light and hear the siren. In a few seconds, it's driving straight towards me. The officers sees me so I jump over another wall and run into that area. It's not very big and the only thing at the bottom is the canal and the high fences of the sewerage works behind it. I'm effectively trapped but the police will have to come in and find me if they want me. I hide behind a large bush, hardly daring to breathe or move a muscle.

The car stops where I have jumped over the wall and the police get out. They have large flashlights and are scouring the area. Eventually they seem to lose interest and leave.

I now think it's unsafe to proceed to Halifax. The whole incident has left me slightly shaken up and having the police involved isn't part of my plan. I decide to make my way back home, but I can't take a chance by using any of the roads where they've seen me. I will have to go back via the canal bank. This runs near my house and I can get off near there.

There's only one small issue. The canal bank is on the opposite side to where I am so the only way to the towpath is through the canal. The depth of the canal isn't the problem as it's only a few feet deep, but I still don't want to draw any attention to myself so I slowly, carefully, lower myself into the canal and wade through it to the other side, then run back home.

I arrive home soaking wet from the chest down, take off my clothes outside the house, go inside and get a plastic bag, bundle the clothes in it and leave the bag over a wall outside the house. I clean myself up and get into bed, cold, tired but exhilarated. I have tangled with the police and won.

I decide to try again to break into the shop again. Previously I have run there in the middle of the night but ended up being chased by the police after they stopped me on the roadside. This time I'll be a little more clever.

I go into Mystendyke after school one day and buy a glasscutter to extract a piece of glass from the front window. This is so much easier and quieter than trying to smash windows with bricks and crowbars. I wait again until Mum gets drunk one night, then proceed to run to Halifax as before, but this time along the canal bank and through the woods, keeping away from the main road. I have learned my lesson.

The shop is in the middle of the town centre. As I approach town I do my best to stay hidden, darting from one building to the next. Outside the shop, I look in to see what's there: to my surprise and delight there is a beautiful patterned Pringle jumper in the window. Quite a few lads at school have Pringle jumpers but none has a top-of-the-range patterned one like this. It's an exclusive, rare, expensive jumper and it will turn the rest of them green with envy.

I can't get started quickly enough with my glasscutter. I carefully mark out a section in the window and try cutting into it. After fifteen minutes of putting my whole weight into this glasscutter, it is obvious it isn't working. I hadn't realized that the shop window has industrial-strength plate glass. My tiny glasscutter is for much thinner glass. I persevere but am still getting nowhere. I finally lose patience: I will never get through the window with this implement and I'm now worried that a police patrol car may be around at any moment. So I revert to my previous method. I find a large stone and throw it through the window. The alarm goes off, piercing the night but I reach in, get the jumper and am off and away.

I run all the way home the same way as I have run into town. This time, unlike my earlier, botched foray into

Halifax, there are no police chases and wading through the canal. I am overjoyed: I have committed another perfect burglary and come away with something worth a lot of money and highly desirable. I tuck the jumper at the bottom of my wardrobe and go to sleep a happy lad.

I don't want to get caught with the stolen goods again so I wait a few weeks before wearing the jumper one weekend in Ludden Bridge. Quite a few lads make comments about it and I feel really good. One lad gets very animated about buying it so I sell it to him. Even though I love the jumper, I know it's stolen and feel a little uncomfortable about wearing it in case questions are asked about where I bought it. I am also concerned about Mum because, despite the fact that she has no idea what a Pringle jumper is, she might question where a brand new, quality jumper like this came from. Besides, the other lad has no idea it was stolen so he isn't going to grass me up.

A short while after I sell it, the police contact Mum and come up to our house to see her. They say that they want to talk to me as well. The interview is extraordinary.

'Mrs Brownstone, we've had reports that David's been stealing and selling stolen goods.'

Mum's mouth hits the floor. After the incident in the paper shop, the suicide attempt and police caution she has assumed it's all behind us.

'Who's said this?' she asks quietly.

'We're not at liberty to say. They say that David sold them a jumper that we now know was stolen from a shop window in Halifax.'

At this point, all eyes turn to me. Mum's look tells me she desperately wants to believe it isn't true. The police officers have a benign expression so I surmise they may not think it's me. I know the lad I've sold the jumper to: he has a bit of form for petty crime, which presents me with an opportunity. If I lie, it will be my word against his.

'Of course I didn't nick it,' I say confidently, with a touch of indignation. 'I know I did the paper shop thing but that's all in the past.' I look the police officers straight in the eye. 'It wasn't me.'

Mum's so relieved I think she's going to pass out. The police also seem to relax as if they've heard what they've expected to hear.

'Well, actually, we didn't think it was you. We know what happened last time and the other lad is well known to us.'

I can't believe my ears. A simple denial has been enough to prove my innocence. I don't know how they've linked the jumper with me or whether the other lad has got into trouble for possessing the jumper but that's it – I hear no more about it. Mum is so relieved that I have denied it and that it wasn't me. Unfortunately the euphoria isn't to last very long.

I have kept a diary in which I have put down everything: dates and times of all the burglaries I have attempted and committed; even my thoughts about where I could burgle next. I come home one day to find Mum seated at the dining table reading it. My face turns purple. I feel angry, embarrassed, upset, and furious with myself for letting her find it. I have hidden it in my bedroom but she's found it. I am annoyed with her too because she can only have found it by making a detailed search of my room. But she now knows all the secrets I really don't want her to know.

Mum is devastated by everything she reads. She can't believe I have lied so blatantly to the police and that they have bought my story. She is stunned that I am still getting up in the middle of the night and running a ten-mile round trip to commit a burglary in the middle of town.

She also asks about the ticks on various pages: there are two lots of ticks. Red ones are when I've had sex with Suzy — as my first proper girlfriend I've wanted to make a note of our sex life. Blue ones are when my mother has approached me for sex.

I tell her the truth about the red ones, but when it comes to the blue ones I feel I have a choice. I can front her out and tell her what's been happening when she's drunk and that they represent the times she has asked me for sex. Or I can lie to her and let her carry on in ignorance. I look at my mother and I lie. I simply don't have it in me to tell her the truth. I tell her that the blue ticks, which are not too many and scattered randomly mainly over the weekend pages, are when Suzy and I have had sex in a new place. She buys my story and never checks it out.

She could destroy my story very easily by tallying the blue ticks with her drinking binges. But she doesn't. I wonder if things might be different from now on if I tell her the truth, that she's an aggressive sexual predator when she's drunk. She might find it within herself to change if she were to receive such a jolt to her nervous system. There can't be many things worse for a woman to hear than that she has tried to have sex with her son while completely off her head on alcohol.

But I think on balance it would only make things worse. She is truly in the grip of the disease of alcoholism and nothing is going to shake it off. However, Mum does surprise me in one respect. Almost all the time she struggles with the most basic of stressful situations. Having a puncture or being late for work can send her into a blind panic. When she discovered the diary and the volatile material it contained I assumed she'd be livid. I keep waiting for the volcano to appear but it never does. For once, she sits me down and talks to me as an equal. Maybe she thinks it too serious for her to do otherwise. So we have a long chat about what's in the diary. I have no choice but to confess to everything I have done. The most recent event involving the jumper is in there and she wants to know all the details.

We also chat about Suzy and sex. As Suzy and I are having an active sex life, as evidenced by the red ticks, Mum and I discuss contraception: she understandably doesn't want me to get Suzy pregnant and, in her words, ruin my life. She finally says she isn't going to report me to the police. As bizarre as that sounds, her strong moral compass and sense of right and wrong mean that it isn't a foregone conclusion that she will not shop me to the authorities.

In many respects Mum believes in tough love and it wouldn't surprised me were she to put me in the car and take me down the police station to confess all. I am mightily relieved when she says she won't do that. We destroy the diary – there are admissions to criminal activities in there and she doesn't want them getting out and I don't start another diary. At the end of our conversation, she pleads with me to stop committing these crimes. She goes through the usual parental routine of telling me what the grave consequences would be if I don't straighten up.

I know I've had another lucky escape. I listen intently and nod, promising I'll never do anything like this again. The problem is, it's now in my system. I am stealing because it gives me a rush that I don't get from anything else in my life. I am making decent money at it too. So unfortunately, I lie to her again and immediately begin organizing my next burglary.

The biggest event of my budding criminal life is yet to come.

11

Master Criminal

*S*uzy has been a steadying influence on me throughout this period. She knows about the burglaries and while I must seem an unstable boyfriend she has stood by me and is good for me. We have a strong sexual relationship which has made me feel more confident and has improved my self-esteem. I go on a barge holiday with her family and she comes with us on a family holiday to Wales. We have sex in the woods like teenagers do when they can't get time alone.

Our relationship is an important part of my life but even after the diary conversation Mum, as ever, tries to interfere. She sits us both down.

'So I guess that you two are now having sex?' she asks nonchalantly.

I want to jump out of the window with embarrassment. 'Mum, do we have to talk about this?'

'Yes, we do. I'm just looking out for the pair of you.'

I look at Suzy and she just grins.

'So what kind of contraception are you using?' Mum continues.

'Right, that's it!' I get up. 'Come on, Suzy, let's go and walk the dogs.'

I know Mum is trying to help and that these things need to be discussed but it simply confuses me. When drunk, she's still asking me for sex at home; when sober she's asking searching, personal questions about sex and offering advice like some kindly old sex-education teacher.

She once walked into my room and caught me masturbating. I was horrified and tried to pull up my trousers as quickly as I could. She calmly turned round and walked out. I waited for ages before going downstairs. Even then I was cringing with embarrassment and knew what was about to come next as I sat down to watch TV. After a deathly silence, Mum could finally no longer contain herself.

'There's nothing wrong with it, David.'

'Nothing wrong with what?'

'Masturbation.'

'Muuummm, do we have to talk about it?'

She proceeded to lecture me on sexual health and keeping my penis clean. It was the worst conversation in the world.

When I can bear to think about it, the questions still besiege me.

Why does she ask me for sex?

What is her trigger for coming to me?

Does she know when she's sober what she does when she's drunk?

Mum's drinking is still of course a big secret. I never discuss it at school with friends or teachers. Mum never drinks when Suzy is at the house so she never knows. I never talked about it to Reg, and Reg never mentions it to me or, as far as I know, anyone else. The problem with this secrecy is that I have no context at all within which to place her drinking and her actions when she is drunk. I am coming up to sixteen and know that what she is doing is wrong. But I don't know *how* wrong because I have nothing to compare it to. If one of my school friends has the same problem with one of their parents they certainly never mention it to me. If they did, then I could talk it through with them and got some kind of alternative perspective on it.

The only time I have seen anyone with a problem similar to Mum's is when we go to visit one of Reg's relatives. Every year we go on a family holiday and apart from the very first when I was seven, it is camping, which I hate with a passion. Waking up with a wet backside, cramped in a tiny tent, having to fetch your own water, share communal showers and cook your food on a gas cooker is about as far away from having fun as my imagination will take me. But we can't afford to go on big holidays abroad or even stay in hotels so there's no choice. We also have dogs which Mum refuses to put in kennels. It's camping or nothing. At least it gets us away from the house and, looking back, I'm glad we've had those holidays.

I'm surprised at Reg. He's almost 75 now but he's still pitching tents like a man half his age. Many retired men would be playing cards all day in a community centre somewhere but he has the strength and willingness to come away on holiday camping with a teenager. He earns some respect off me for that.

One of the biggest benefits of the holidays is that Mum never drinks. When it comes to choosing destinations, we often visit relatives, usually on her side of the family. With my maternal grandparents having many siblings between them, it means that Mum has cousins all over the place.

She keeps in touch with all of them and over the ten-year period since we went to live with Reg, we've met all of them, either through visiting them or their coming to us.

One relation of Reg's we go to see is a woman called Jane. She's a generation below Reg, closer to Mum's age, but I think they are stepbrother and stepsister. Jane is married to Don and they run a chicken business. We go to stay on a campsite near their chicken farm. This farm is different from anything I've come across before. The chickens are in sheds in what looks like cramped conditions but I have no social conscience about this. I am interested in the process and can't believe this is where we get our meat from. The chickens are brought in as chicks only a few days old, fed and watered in huge sheds and then taken away to be slaughtered at three months. They will never see the light of day or wander in a field.

As a child I enjoy doing the morning rounds where we looked for the dead chickens. When a chicken dies, all the others peck it to see what's wrong with it and it ends up being a right mess. This doesn't bother me. I even like it when Don finds a half-dead chicken and has to put it between his knees and strangle it. Fascinated as I am in the whole thing, I'm keen to help out doing any jobs and shadowing Don and I'm thus able to see first hand that Don is a heavy drinker like my mother.

From the moment he enters the chicken shed on the morning of our very first day, he will find a bottle tucked away in a hiding place, have a swig and then will continue drinking all the time he's away from the main house. Whether he's feeding the birds, clearing out the dead ones or filleting one for tea, he always has a bottle nearby.

'Say nothing to Auntie Jane or your Mum and Grandad about the whisky,' he says. 'It's a secret between you and me.'

It seems clear to me Jane knows about his drinking but I'm too young to understand what effect it's having on their relationship. However, when we leave, there is one telling comment. Don is an emotional person who always wears his heart on his sleeve. He's delighted to have us there and is good company. He is obviously going to miss us when we leave. So when we go to see Jane and Don for the last time, Don finds it too much to wish us goodbye and wanders off into the chicken sheds with a wave and a tear in his eye. It's an emotional moment but Jane quickly kills it.

'Don't worry about him. Those are only crocodile tears,' she says dismissively and a little harshly.

To me it's a strange-sounding phrase but reveals a lot. Although Don feels he is keeping his drinking separate, it looks to me to be badly affecting his marriage.

This trip gives me a fresh perspective on Mum's drinking. They have no children, so it's difficult to compare exactly, but I come away feeling that Mum's drinking isn't so bad. At least she doesn't drink early in the morning like Don. She never has bottles hidden all over the place and certainly doesn't have that permanently glazed, ruddy-faced expression Don has that comes with heavy drinking.

Of course, I'm kidding myself. Mum's drinking is heavy when she drinks and she completely loses control of what she says and does. And the damage she does to me emotionally through her actions when she is drunk is always there. This is to be brought into sharp relief when her past comes back to haunt her, which comes about from a very positive action on her part.

* * *

'David, I've got something to tell you,' Mum says one day. She looks excited, agitated even. 'I've found your grandfather.' She blurts it out as if she were telling me she'd won the lottery.

My first thoughts are that she's talking about *her* father who died five years ago but as Mum isn't into the whole spiritual other-worldly stuff I quickly twig that she means my dad's father.

I think that is fantastic. Grandparents tend to be children's favourite relatives and that is so with me. I loved Mum's dad very much. My grandmother – Dad's mum – is still alive and although strange and eccentric, I think she's cool too. To meet my paternal grandfather is going to be amazing. I have no idea how she has found him or even if she's been in touch with him all along. But she has initiated contact and then told me.

It's strange though: this granddad has never been mentioned before in my life. He's been the great unspoken invisible person in our family and it's never occurred to me to ask about him. My relationship with Dad has always been impersonal and he's never brought him up. Conversation and correspondence between Dad and me is weak anyway and his dad is never going to crop up in a casual chat.

But I'm surprised that Mum has never mentioned him. She often talks about family, especially her parents. Even though my maternal grandmother died before I was born,

Mum occasionally mentions her and I knew my maternal grandfather before he died when I was ten. I just assume there's a reason he's never been mentioned, even though I don't know what it is.

It's also a mystery why she hasn't contacted him before now. Maybe it's the death of her own father just a few months ago that's been the trigger. One thing is clear from his early letters though. Mum seems to want Grandad to get to know me and have a 'meaningful relationship' with me.

In one of his first letters in October 1979, which he writes just to Mum, he is obviously intrigued that Mum has written to him but a little wary about the reasons for her doing so:

Thinking about the purpose of your letter, it is difficult to know how it is possible to have any sort of meaningful relationship with David. He could hardly be expected to evince much interest in a grey-haired old man full of all sorts of 'itis-es'! You don't want a list, I'm sure; suffice it so say there are not too many hours when some sort of pain doesn't rear its ugly head. A very dull grandad, I fear. Couldn't even kick a football around without paying up for it.

Incidentally, you mention his grandmother – does he see her? Ever or often? How is she? What are her circumstances? Do you have her address? You know, Carol, you'd make a good lawyer. You only let people know what you want them to know.

As interesting as it may be that he wants to know how Grandma is, and his revealing comment about Mum, I'm only interested in what he might have to say to me – especially after he starts writing messages directly to me. He's every kid's dream grandfather – interested and very, very funny. He seems to understand what makes a young lad tick; he knows what to say, what I might be interested in. He has energy and passion, which comes through clearly in his letters. He writes mainly to Mum but will add messages just for me:

> *Thank you for your two letters, David. You didn't say what position you played in rugby. You'll have to get tough and eat steak & eggs every morning for breakfast!*
>
> *So you've taken up guitar lessons! Poor Mum! Yes – I was top in French & Maths, but I disliked History. All note-taking & Kings & dates. Ugh.*

We quickly build up this incredible bond. Then we speak to him.

He talks like people do who know how to build rapport. He's interested as well as interesting. He asks about my interests. He instinctively knows what's important to me. He shows more interest in these things in one conversation than Mum, Dad and Reg have ever shown. The phone conversations only increase my anticipation of meeting him. I don't have to wait too long. Even though we're going camping to see him, I'm looking forward to this trip. We pack our trailer and set off for Worcester where he lives with his sister Dorothy. We stop at a beautiful campsite not too far from his house.

On the way to meeting him, I am beside myself with excitement. As we pull up outside his house, it isn't entirely as I imagined. It's small and plain. Somehow I have pictured a much bigger place, something to match his huge personality. We get out of the car and go down the garden path. Before we have even knocked on the door, he's standing there with a smile as wide as his face.

'Hello David, I'm your Grandad.'

My immediate feeling is disappointment. The man in the letters was energetic and dashing. The man standing in front of me is old, without much hair; what is left is white. He has a slight stoop like many old people and seems to shuffle rather than walk. But his eyes shine and soon he dispels all my doubts and shows me he can be the grandparent in the letters and more.

There isn't a moment I spend with Grandad that is less than fantastic. He's funny and interesting. He tells stories with flair and detail. His sister, Dorothy, though, is different: a very kind-looking person who constantly has a smile on her face, but more reserved.

The inside of their house is austere. Mum has mentioned that they belong to the Plymouth Brethren, a strict Christian evangelical religious movement. The religious side doesn't bother her as she's been a lifelong churchgoer at the local Methodist church in Mystendyke, and I have also gone to church from a very young age, including Sunday school and prayer meetings. I have always taken religion at face value. To me it's a social event. I've also been in the church play every year and enjoy rehearsing for it. I still go to church with Mum and appreciate it as something we do together.

It isn't until much later in my life that I will question my belief and become an atheist: while respecting other people's beliefs I don't believe in God myself.

But at the age of 16 I know nothing of the Plymouth Brethren other than their members are devout Christians who follow the Bible very closely, even literally. Because of their religious membership, Grandad and Dorothy have no television and their house has no frills or luxuries. They believe in living a simple Christian life although at one point my Grandad does describe life as being quite 'samey'. This basic approach to life only adds to the impact of his personality. He is such wonderful company to be around and I find myself regarding him as a shining light in my life.

* * *

After Mum has read my diaries, I tell her I will cease all criminal activity, despite my history. So far I have committed multiple burglaries which she knows all about. I have been caught for one and received a police caution. I have done another and the police have ended up at our house. All this while I have been lying to Mum every step of the way about what I was really doing. For me, it's all one big game. I have failed on several occasions and actually attempted suicide on the back of it. But I'm feeling a lot stronger emotionally now, and ready and raring to go again. I feel better prepared to perform the burglaries, more confident that I can pull them off. I decide to raise the stakes and therefore plan my most ambitious burglary to date.

Because of my passion for sports clothes, I always find myself in stores selling every kind of sports clothing available including Lacoste clothing, my favourite and most expensive. This is what I want to get my hands on as it confers immediate status on those schoolkids who wear it. Problem is, I can't afford it so I decide to steal it instead.

Tell Me Why, Mummy

I single out my next target and as always, I'll break in in the middle of the night. But logistics are a problem. I am committing my crimes when Mum is in a deep drink-induced sleep. Being comatose means there is nothing she can do to stop it happening and she has no way of knowing while under the influence of alcohol.

But my next burglary will be different from the others. It is a full train journey away from my house; no trains run in the middle of the night. I can't get there after she has gone to sleep and be back before she wakes up. Then an opportunity presents itself out of the blue that is too perfect to be true. Mum wants to go to Worcester to visit Grandad. But the time when she wants to go clashes with some important school exams for me. Unbelievably, and despite everything that has happened, she decided to go anyway with Reg, leaving me home alone. We agree that I'll do my exams and follow on afterwards by train.

I can't believe my luck – a heaven-sent chance to carry out the burglary. I check out the shop a few days before they are due to leave. Amazingly, they have a large display of Lacoste clothes in the shop window – exactly what I'm after. I'm so excited in the days leading up to this. I plan every aspect down to the last detail. I know it's going to work out fine, plus I'm going to be getting clothes that I desperately want and that everyone else will be so jealous of.

I tell Suzy about my plans. Although she doesn't encourage me or want to get involved, she has no moral qualms. For the two nights leading up to 'my trip', Suzy stays with me at the house. This is really cool in itself: it feels great to have the house without Reg and Mum there. I invite a mate to stop one night who also has a girlfriend from Blackholme and they sleep in one of the other bedrooms. We have a ball.

On the big night, Suzy and I are at my house. As planned, I am catching the last train so I can spend more time with her and so I can't bottle out and change my mind. Whether I do the burglary or not, I'll be stuck in another town all night until the first train leaves around 6 am. I take her home to Blackholme, make my way to the station, get a ticket and board the last train. I have a large sports bag with me and an iron bar, having learned that the easiest way to smash through a plate-glass window is with something big and heavy. An hour later I am in the town centre. It is still busy with plenty of people around as you'd expect, even at that time of night. I go straight to the store to have a look. The Lacoste display is still there. I can barely contain myself with excitement.

I decide not to attract attention to myself. The best idea would be to lie low until the town is really quiet. I find a quiet spot in the grounds of an office complex and try to get some sleep. At about 3 am I set off for the store. The town is eerily quiet; no-one is around, including any police. Perfect. It feels exactly the same as when I've broken into the shop in Halifax in the middle of the night.

I am careful to walk in the shadows and where I think there'll be no police. I know an open shopping complex and decide to walk through there. The bright lights of the shops make me conspicuous but I figure I'll be out of sight. There is only one way in and one way out. As I am walking through, I hear a loud sound. It isn't close but it surprises me. I have a quick look behind me, see nothing and carry on walking. I turn a corner to find a police officer walking towards me.

My heart leaps into my mouth and I feel myself starting to panic. What shall I do? I'm not doing anything wrong so I decide to carry on walking towards him. If I turn round, he'll surely give chase. Just as I get to him, he stops me.

'What are you making all that noise for?' he asks accusingly.

'It wasn't me,' I reply truthfully, desperately trying not to look like I'm off to commit a burglary.

He eyes me up and down suspiciously. As a police officer, he must be wondering what on earth a young lad is doing walking round the centre of town in the middle of the night carrying a large holdall.

'What's in the bag, lad?'

He puts his hand out and I know I'll have to make a run for it. I am much fitter than him and think it's simply a question of outrunning him as I've done with the police officers before. I set off for the entrance of the shopping centre as quickly as I can. The cover I have wanted from the shopping centre is now going to go against me. If a copper appears in front of me I'll be trapped.

I can hear him chasing me while talking into his radio. I'm not overly worried as I assume that cover will be low for the middle of the night, but as I bolt out of the shopping centre I see another police officer running towards me from a different direction. I manage to evade him and get out in the open, then run the opposite way to the two now chasing me. But as I run, police appear from every angle. They are narrowing down my options and eventually I run down an alleyway. Unfortunately, it's a dead end.

I look for cover and hide behind some bins at the bottom of some steps, praying the police haven't seen me coming down the alleyway.

No such luck. They all know where I am and convene at the end, getting their breath back. They slowly walk down shining their torches into all the nooks and crannies. Eventually they come to the steps and shine their torches down at me.

'Come on up, son, we can see you,' one officer says, still out of breath.

I feel like a caged animal and don't want to give myself up. In a moment of madness, I open the holdall, grab the iron bar and throw away the bag. I come up the steps with the bar behind my back. As I get to the top, an officer starts to pull his handcuffs out. I run towards him with the iron bar, swinging with all my strength and aiming squarely at the side of his head.

Fortunately, he moves slightly at the last second and I catch him on the side of his body, but the force of my attack still knocks him over. If he hadn't moved and I'd made full contact, I could have killed him. In a flash, the police grab me and throw me to the floor face down. One sits on my back, another handcuffs me. But I know this isn't going to end here.

As I lie there, my face being ground into the dirt, I am struggling to breathe. I turn my head to one side to get some air and just as I do, one of the officers comes up and takes a penalty kick using my face as a football. I scream with agony and my face explodes. Immediately, my eye and mouth are filled with blood and dirt, making my breathing even worse, because my mouth is blocked and they are pinning me down. I am really panicking, thinking they're going to let me suffocate here and now.

They see I'm in trouble and pick me up. I can see the hatred in their eyes. They know I have intended to injure or even fatally hurt one of their colleagues. Now it is their turn to get their own back. They step forward and give me a beating. I have handcuffs on, otherwise I would defend myself and with force, for I am in a place where I really don't give a shit. I just want to be able to hit one of them back and if I could get those cuffs off there's nothing I wouldn't do. I am way out of control and would love to put the bastard copper in hospital who's kicked me in the face.

I love a ruck and don't even care if I get hurt. An all-out fight with a bunch of coppers would be the biggest rush of all. I'm in a mess now, with blood all over my face and clothes. I'm struggling with my breathing and can't see out of one eye where one of them has kicked me. I have also shit myself. Anyone seeing me at this moment wouldn't recognize me. But it could be worse: they've punched me in the stomach but not in the face. The only facial injury I have is a bad cut above one eye which causes huge bleeding. Mum will certainly have seen the cut – it is to leave a minor scar for the rest of my life – but I never tell her and she never asks me. In any event, she would never complain to the authorities but would say that I am receiving my just desserts. She can be a hard cow when she wants to be but on this occasion she is absolutely right. I've nearly killed a police officer and I get all that I deserve in return. They are right to do what they did to me.

They take me to the station where they throw me in a cell before interviewing me. It occurs to me that apart from assaulting the officer, a serious enough crime in itself, I have done nothing wrong. Maybe resisting arrest but I haven't stolen anything and so haven't committed any crime of that kind. I'm going to get into enough trouble as it is without admitting to something I haven't actually done. So I decide to lie through my teeth. It has worked before and will work again.

Two officers take me into an interview room and sit me down. They look at me as if I were a complete waste of space.

'So, what are you doing in town tonight?'

'Nothing,' I reply, as if it were perfectly normal behaviour to be walking around town at 3 am.

'Look, son, we know you are going equipped to do something. You might as well tell us what it is.'

'And when you go in front of a judge,' the second officer jumps in, 'he's not going to look at it any differently. So cough up and save us all a lot of time and trouble.'

My strategy is immediately blown out of the water. How did they know I was going to burgle a shop? Then it slowly dawns on me that these aren't valley cops, dealing with petty crime, like the ones in Ludden Bridge where I have sold my stolen jumper, but highly experienced cops who can read a situation like a book. I change my tack and confess all.

They charge me and put me back in the cell. My charge is 'going equipped to steal' or something like that. Bizarrely, they never charge me for assaulting the officer. They have certainly had their pound of flesh in the alleyway and got their own back but it surprises me nonetheless. Maybe if they'd done so it would have shone a brighter light on my injuries. It is easy to see they are not the normal injuries sustained during the course of an arrest.

I spend the rest of the night in the cell, contemplating my actions and, more importantly, what Mum is going to say once she finds out, although, to be honest, I couldn't care less. In the morning I have to wait for Social Services to come and escort me out because I am under 16. I make my way home, sort myself out, then phone Mum. She is understandably angry, but instead of hotfooting it back from Worcester, she decides to stay there and wait for me to turn up.

I get picked up from the train station at Worcester by Mum and Grandad. She says nothing and we set off towards the campsite. Eventually, Grandad breaks the silence.

'Your mother's been very worried about you,' he says, stating the obvious.

I'm now becoming oblivious to criticism or concern and say nothing. I just stare out of the window and the rest of the holiday passes in a strained silence.

* * *

Mum is having trouble dealing with everyday life. She soon stops working and will never work again purely due to stress. This makes home life even more volatile as she is able to drink even more. Of course, my criminal activities don't help as they distress her deeply. We argue constantly as she pushes me to tell her why I am doing it. I tell her I don't know but underneath I feel I'm not completely to blame.

The sexual activity and demands over a ten-year period have left my head in a real mess. Inside I am shouting at her. I want to say that the way I felt when I was stealing and selling the stuff was the way I should have felt being her son – special, important, the centre of attention. I want to scream in her face:

Don't you know that you ask me to fuck you every time you get pissed?

Don't you know that for ten years you've messed up my head and this is how I've turned out?

Why don't you accept some responsibility?

It's all your fault, you selfish bitch!

But whenever I open my mouth to utter the words, nothing comes out. Instead, as always, I try to pacify her and make her happy. I tell her I won't do it any more but I don't know myself exactly what's going to happen. The assault on the police officer has shown me that I'm on the ragged edge. Anything's possible. Each event is escalating in terms of violence and potential outcome.

There's still the question of a court appearance. This last burglary meant I was going to end up in court and would definitely receive a juvenile criminal conviction. A court welfare officer attended our home and had to carry out an evaluation of me and my home life to assist the judge with sentencing.

I attend the juvenile criminal court on 31 July 1984. Mum and Reg come and I am smartly dressed in jacket, shirt and tie. I tell the Judge I want to join the Armed Forces and serve the community. It's a load of rubbish but it sounds good.

The court welfare report says that I come from an excellent background with good parents. If only they knew. Consequently, the Judge gives me a two-year conditional discharge. This means that nothing is going to happen to me for the next two years, but if I commit any more crimes in this period I will suffer a very serious penalty. I can't believe my ears. I am being let off again. I just have to keep my nose clean and I'll suffer no punishment.

This run of events is bizarre and deeply ironic. I have received a very lenient sentence in light of the stable family background the Judge thinks I have when in fact it's the very thing that's almost certainly a huge contributory factor to my committing the crimes in the first place.

But even though I've been very fortunate in court, something has changed in me. I decide to stop committing any more burglaries. I have no idea what the trigger is for such a complete change of heart, but I feel brilliant for doing it. It is not religious or anything that Mum has said. I don't even feel remorse. I think I just want to do something with my life. It has been an exciting, rollercoaster ride but I understand that there are moral and ethical issues involved in criminal activity. I have reached the point where I feel uncomfortable stealing other people's property and am old enough to understand that it is going to start affecting my life big time if I don't stop right now.

I appreciate that I've got off very lightly with the court. They have given me yet another chance. It is definitely time to call it a day on my criminal career.

* * *

In the middle of all this madness I sit my O-level exams to decide my whole future. Mum desperately wants me to stay on at school and do A levels so I can go to university or college. I'm not naturally academic so going into the sixth form is always going to be a challenge. But she gives me no option. I scrape through five passes and although none is an A grade, I pass enough to go into the sixth form – but only just.

Life is changing for the better in some key areas. Mum's drinking hasn't improved but I feel better able to handle it and have passed my exams well enough to give me a chance of some kind of career. I have turned my back on the criminal stuff and I still have Suzy. Throughout all my problems of the previous six months she has been my rock and has stood by me. She has also transferred schools and come to mine to continue her education. We will now be seeing each other almost every day, which makes me very happy. I feel better about life and am positive about the future.

I return to school in September. Everyone knows about what I have done and about my appearance in court. I tell them all I'm not going to do it any more and that I am finished with stealing.

I have only been back a couple of days when I get a call to go to the Deputy Headmaster's office. The last time I was summoned like this was when I robbed the paper shop and threw myself in front of a car. As I walk to the office I wonder what it could be about – maybe my court appearance, but that was a couple of months ago. If he does mention it I will tell him that I won't be doing this crazy stuff any more, that I've learned my lesson. I turn down the same corridor as a few months ago and knock on his door.

'Come in,' he says.

'You wanted to see me, sir.'

'Yes, David, please sit down.'

I sit on a chair. He perches on the edge of his table.

'I believe you've been to court this summer and received a juvenile criminal conviction,' he says sternly.

'Yes, sir,' I reply. 'It was for something that happened a few months ago.'

'Well, as you know, you've had a series of run-ins with the law over the last six months and, consequently, I'm going to expel you from this school.'

I feel like I've been hit with a hammer. I can't understand why I'm getting expelled. Kids like me don't get expelled. Really naughty, deviant kids get expelled.

'But … but, sir, I know I've done wrong but that's all in the past now,' I stutter, not quite believing what I'm hearing.

He looks at me and his tone hardens. 'I don't care. You've been a lot of trouble to this school for quite some time. You've had your chance and it's now time for somewhere else to have to put up with you.'

With that, I empty my locker and leave the school for good. Shortly after this, my mother receives a letter from the school:

David has made promises about his conduct which he has broken and we think he will be a disturbing influence on the Sixth Form.

When I see it written in black and white it really brings home what I have actually done.

* * *

Getting expelled devastates me. Maybe it's because it's a school I've known for so many years. Or maybe because Suzy had come to the same school as me. Not that this matters too much: shortly afterwards, we go to a house party and she gets off with someone else and dumps me. After all we've gone through and all the fantastic support she's given me, she goes off with someone else.

I'm shattered and lonely and I've started to realize the true implications of what I've done. It hasn't occurred to me that my actions might have lifelong and far-reaching consequences.

12

On the Scrapheap

After going to court, being expelled from school and being dumped by Suzy, I'm at a low ebb. I'm not motivated to further my studies or indeed to do anything. I have no close friends to speak of as all my previous ones have been people I've knocked about with at school. However, I'm used to being by myself and don't mind this too much. Mum is upset about my expulsion and tells me it's all my own doing, but after that she is proactive in moving me on.

There are few consolations about finding myself well and truly on the scrapheap, but one thing I do like doing is getting a Day Rover, a one-price ticket allowing unlimited travel by bus and train anywhere within West Yorkshire. It's relatively cheap and means I can hop on and off the public transport system at will, going anywhere I like. The freedom is fantastic. I can go out for the whole day for a relatively small amount of money and often go somewhere new and different, like Batley, just for the hell of it.

But even though I now have no school to go to, Mum pushes me, saying I should do my A levels elsewhere or I'll never get a job. There's also a second incentive. If you're aged between 16 and 18 and don't have a job, you have to go on a YTS, a Youth Training Scheme, a government initiative to work around the idea of giving young unemployed people the skills to get employment. In reality, it's slave labour as they only pay around £30 a week and it's really designed to keep the unemployment figures down.

So I start doing A levels at my local college. One of the topics I'm studying is French. I like it and my spoken French is pretty good, mainly because I've been on two French exchanges and have spent many hours writing letters in French to my exchange counterpart. But there's only three of us signed up for the French A level so they can it. Three weeks after I start, I decide to leave the college and try elsewhere as I want to do French.

I know I'll be stuck with a YTS job if I don't find somewhere to do my A levels so I think I'd better approach some more schools and decide to go for one of the best school in Halifax – Hunter and Maxwell, a grammar school with an amazing reputation, producing fantastic results and Oxbridge candidates every year. It is highly academic and disciplined. Without even a phone call, let alone an interview, I turn up at the school and ask if I can sign up. The Deputy Head takes me into her office and we have a brief chat. She asks why I've left my previous school. I lie, not daring to tell her I've been expelled. I feed her a line about how good this school is, how I want to better myself. She swallows it.

I start a few days later and immediately realize it's a huge mistake. From day one I'm so far out of my depth I feel like I'm on a different planet inhabited by superstudents. Ludden High was a completely different kind of school, a typical comprehensive with the majority of kids not getting five O levels or more. At Hunter and Maxwell 99% of kids got five O levels or more; over 95% go on to do A levels. All the way through the sixth form, one thing highlights the difference between the two schools. At Ludden High students discussed whether they were going to pass their exams, hoping they would get enough. At Hunter and Maxwell, they assume they'll pass; it's just a question of what grades they're going to get.

It's obvious I am going to have to work at a much higher level than ever before to pass these exams, produce results previously beyond me, and focus seriously on my weaknesses to give myself the best chance. I do none of these things. The volume of homework overwhelms me. The difference between O and A levels is too great for me to bridge. I'm gobsmacked at the speed at which other students effortlessly seem to learn new information. All this is multiplied many times by the social aspect of the school.

Even though this is a non-fee paying school, it's one of a very few traditional grammar schools in the Halifax area out of many secondary schools. There is still an entrance exam kids have to take at eleven and special buses come from as far away as Lancashire and Derbyshire bringing in students, such is its reputation. Naturally, most of the students are from the top of the socio-economic spectrum. Their parents are mainly professional people with money.

I just don't fit in. It doesn't help that I've entered at sixth-form level. Everyone else in my year doing A levels has known each other for five years and they've got many settled and developed relationships. I'm on the outside looking in. But I don't leave, and over time I do get to make a few friends as everyone does.

My main friend is Simon. He isn't in my form but does a couple of my lessons. He's a trendy dresser, with curly hair, slim but in good shape. He's friendly with other kids but usually sits on his own; a social butterfly able to get on with many people but also comfortable on his own. He's funny, switched on, quick-witted and very likable. We get on well and become good mates. It's a pleasure to have him as a friend but I always feel like I'm playing second fiddle to him. He's very fit, has the gift of the gab and plays for the school rugby team, which is a great honour for boys at this school. He never has a problem getting a girlfriend. They are always nice looking and I often look on in envy, wondering what it must be like to be in that position.

After Suzy, I have another girlfriend in Blackholme but that only lasts a short while. During the two years I'm at my new school I have several girlfriends, but they tend to have led much more sheltered lives. They are either quiet and shy or from a year or two below me. As a teenager who's anxious to discover more about sex, none of this adds to my confidence, but a couple of things happen that are to change that.

The first is acting in the school play. A teacher asks me to be in it and I'm so delighted to have been asked that I say yes without quite realizing what it entails. I play Benvolio in the school production of *Romeo and Juliet*. I enjoy it and being on stage is thrilling. The teacher knows how to get the best out of me and I get stuck into it.

Out of my performance comes the chance to go out with a girl called Jeanine. She is tall, confident, good looking and oozes sex appeal, someone I'd have previously considered out of my league. She sees me in the play and asks me out. I must have done something to impress her. We go out for a short while and then I do something stupid.

Mum wants to visit Grandad in Worcester, but as Reg doesn't want to go, I have to accompany her. Because of her previous liaison with Grandad, albeit twenty years before, Reg doesn't want her going alone. I have only been seeing Jeanine a short time and don't want to leave her for a week during a school holiday, but Mum insists.

Upon returning to school, one of Jeanine's friends asks me how my week has gone. Ridiculously, I tell her I've been with another girl in Worcester. I have no idea at all why I've said this or what I expect to achieve from it, except of course to make me seem like someone in demand. Of course, there's only one possible outcome. By the end of the day, Jeanine's friend has told her and she's dumped me. She's certainly been the best-looking girl-friend I have ever had and I lose her over something that has never actually happened.

I also get to know a lad called Tim. A slim, dark-haired lad, he's a year younger than me but lives near me and catches the same bus back. He's quiet, distant and enig-matic and our friendship is slow to build, but I'm intrigued by him and by what makes him tick.

My school life is, as always, full of teenage angst, inse-curity and adolescent hormones. I find it all a struggle: mainly from lack of confidence in knowing what to say and do. In that respect, I am probably no different from most teenagers. But unlike some, my insecurities are not helped by life at home.

* * *

Reg is now 76 and Mum effectively his carer. He is able to get round perfectly fine but she has to take a greater role in looking after him and the house. He now plays no part in my life at all. He isn't there to support or help in any way. He could still easily do so by offering the odd word of advice or encouragement. A small word here or there could make a big difference. He is still my only real paternal influence and, as such, could give his perspective on things for me in the same way as many people learn from their grandparents.

But it isn't to be. He hardly speaks a word to me. I operate independently of Reg. I am self-sufficient, getting myself everywhere I need to be on my own as Mum will never take me in the car. Reg isn't involved in the decision-making process with me. If I need permission to go somewhere, I ask Mum and she'll make a unilateral decision. I mostly feed myself apart from Sunday when we have roast dinner together. Reg and Mum prepare it, allowing her to feel we are a family unit and that sharing a Sunday meal proves it.

There is now an extra problem: Mum stopped working at 43 because of stress. Many people who have never suffered debilitating stress scoff at the idea that you cannot work because of it. But some people can get so stressed over the smallest thing that it simply swamps them. This is the case with Mum. There are a huge number of small, everyday incidents that can do just this like a door being left open or someone saying something out of turn. I can only imagine how she struggled to work with other people where she would have needed to use tact and diplomacy to get what she wanted. These are not her greatest personal skills. She browbeats us into submission to get her own way and I think she must have found it difficult not being able to do exactly what she wanted at work.

It cannot have helped that I have gone off the rails in my teens. A suicide attempt, assaulting a police officer, multiple burglaries, a court appearance and being expelled from school would have a serious impact on any parent but particularly Mum who just doesn't have the ability to deal with it. Once stressed, she will often react by getting drunk. I can never work out whether the stress caused her to drink or whether she needs the drink to remove the stress.

'I've had a really stressful day, I must have a drink,' she'll say, before disappearing to the off licence in her car.

A few hours later she'll be smashed, banging on my door, demanding sex, wandering all over the house, trying to cook food. As always, I'll be there by her side, keeping an eye on her, suffering the verbal and sometimes physical abuse that will come my way until eventually she goes to bed. Now she has finished working, these incidents become more frequent. She has always been careful not to drink when she's working next day. It's only done on a weekend. But now she can drink any time she wants to. There is nothing to hold her back.

* * *

Patience is a virtue I am blessed with to deal with Mum in these moments. But many other people don't have that blessing. Like my Grandad. We have been having steady contact with him for six years. We have been down to Worcester to see him a few times and have developed a strong bond with him. I love him and have fallen for his charm and humour. After Mum's constantly erratic behaviour and Reg's complete indifference to me, being with Grandad is pure joy.

He certainly likes to share. When he visits our house, he splashes out on a brand new fridge for us. Mum is ecstatic. Most of our white goods are secondhand from the local paper. It's wonderful to have something brand new although it does look out of place in our rather spartan kitchen.

When his sister Dorothy suddenly dies, we don't go to the funeral but we do continue to see Grandad after that. Although he is deeply saddened at losing his sister, I think it does release him and makes him even more exuberant. He even buys a television, something Dorothy said they'd never have. Even though both Grandad and his sister have been very religious people, attending church every week and donating a small but significant percentage of their income to the Plymouth Brethren, it is clear that Dorothy has been more devout than her brother.

I sense there's even more to come from him and am looking forward to developing my relationship with him. But then it stops. In an instant. Like so many relationships Mum has been in before, it follows a pattern. She will initiate contact, develop it further, take it to the point where she is close to the other person then destroy it.

Years later I find the letters from Grandad when Mum re-established contact, which shed new light for me on their relationship. The first two, after she wrote to him in 1979, say she should be careful about what she writes as Dorothy reads all his letters. In November he writes:

You might like to know that Dorothy reads all my letters.
There really isn't anything I can do, is there?

And a month later:

By the way, whatever you may write in the future, do
remember that Dorothy & I share all letters (except the one
Keith wrote to me). She is & always has been, a very loving
& godly woman. So very different from her renegade
relative.

And certainly the tone of the letters changes significantly
after Dorothy died some years later. They aren't explicit
in any way, more playful and suggestive.

I am also under the impression that Dad hadn't known
about the contact we were having with Grandad from
whom he'd been estranged for many years. However, Mum
eventually told Dad who was obviously upset about it. A
letter from Grandad gently berates Mum for telling him,
implying that he didn't need to know. He is also exasper-
ated that Dad feels this way:

I hate pomposity. What's Keith got to be pompous about
anyway? We're all jolly good fellows till we're all found
out.

He also implies that something significant happened years
previously causing my Dad to stop seeing him for good,
though he doesn't say what it was. Mum has indicated that
it was because of a fling she'd had with Grandad. She first
tells me this in my teenage years and repeats it many years
later in the presence of someone else.

In October 1983 Grandad wrote that he couldn't believe that Grandma, his wife of 30 years from whom he'd been separated for many years but not divorced, was into Satanism. Of course I knew she was a little weird as she was giving me books on Transcendental Meditation but I hadn't realized that it extended to Satanism. I don't know if Mum embroidered the truth to make it sound more dramatic or if she knew something I didn't but my Grandad's letter was quite clear.

There is nothing in Grandad's last letter, dated November 1985, to indicate why there is no more contact after that. He may have died as he has constantly been ill (he gives regular health updates in every letter), but Mum has certainly never told me he's passed away. I still don't know why we never see, hear from or speak to him again or whether even he's still alive. But one thing's for sure. Mum is the reason and it would be a safe bet to say that her drinking has something to do with it.

But she isn't the only one prone to strange behaviour. Things are also getting weirder with my grandmother.

* * *

I am now going to see Grandma on my own. There is no pressure from Mum but I love her and want to see her, even though she is now more distant and withdrawn. She regards everyone and everything with deep suspicion. Sometimes I find it hard to get into her house and will often have to go through the same ritual. Upon arriving, I knock on her front door.

'Who is it?' she'll shout, from the other side of the locked door.

'It's me, David,' I shout back.

There is a pause while she works out if it's really me, followed by clunks and clicks. She has many locks on the doors and is working her way down them. The door slowly opens a few inches and I can see a safety chain or maybe two on the door, holding it in place so it opens no further. I am careful to resist the natural temptation to put my head in the gap as I know she doesn't like this.

'Hiya, Grandma,' I say in a calm voice.

'Is that you, David?'

'Yes, Grandma, it's me.'

She puts her head in the gap of the door, checking me out. I smile at her. She rarely smiles back but she will then let me in. This happens every time I go to see her. It never worries me particularly because she has always been strange. But there is one incident that shows there might be more to it than eccentricity.

I used to visit Welsdon Barracks for judo lessons with school as part of our PE lesson. Auntie Mavis and Uncle Gerald live nearby. Mavis is actually my great aunt because she's Grandma's sister. She and Gerald are great. The moment I knock on the door, Mavis bounces through the kitchen to let me in. She always gives me a big hug and a kiss. There is never a time when she is anything less than delighted to see me. She knows how to make me feel special.

Gerald is fantastic too. He is funny and solid and has the best job in the world for a kid. He works at a huge chocolate factory in Halifax. The reason this is fantastic is because he comes home every night with bags of seconds chocolate: they taste like the normal bars but don't look as good as they should so they can't be packaged and sold in the shops. It's every child's dream.

We don't buy a lot of chocolate at home because it's expensive in relation to eating home-made sweet stuff. But the moment I step through the door, Mavis will make me milky coffee in a pan on the cooker and give me a plate of chocolate piled high. This is heaven and I love going up there. Mavis and Gerald have no enemies. No-one has a bad word to say about them and they have a very loyal family with one son and two granddaughters. They are the salt of the earth. Then one day, after my customary coffee and chocolate, instead of the usual banter peppered with Mavis's laughter, they go quiet and I can see they're looking quite serious.

'David, we've something to tell you,' says Gerald.

'What?' I forget about the coffee and chocolates as I can tell it's something important and Mavis is looking very upset.

'Your grandma has disowned Mavis.'

'What do you mean?'

'Your grandma has been in touch and says she believes Mavis isn't her sister and that she never wants to hear from her again.'

I'm stunned. Even for Grandma this is bizarre in the extreme. It's also absurd and ridiculous. Mavis and Grandma are in their seventies and always look like two peas from the same pod – their physical similarity is striking. Dad and their son Josh have grown up together and have been to each other's weddings. This is way beyond a joke and is deeply hurtful.

Mavis is devastated but has no choice but to respect Grandma's request to stay away. For me, it's a turning point. To do this, on top of her strange behaviour with me when I visit, is clear evidence that she must have some kind of mental-health issues. But I'm just a kid, watching all this going on around me. I feel for Mavis but never mention to Grandma what they've said. Besides, I myself am still exhibiting some alarming behaviour at times.

* * *

I enjoy being reckless and extreme and rebelling against authority. I've joined the ATC, the Air Training Corps, which is designed to give an insight into what life is like for those interested in joining the Armed Forces. I am kicked out after a couple of months after hitting one of the junior officers who tries to get me to do something I don't want to do.

I am still doing karate and getting good at it. After spending ten years as a cub and scout, I join the Venture Scouts. I do a demonstration for the group one evening, explaining how to punch and kick properly. I then proceed to the pub where I punch the wall in the toilet. I'm on my own at the time and have no idea why I've done it but I leave knuckle-sized marks in the plaster and am later reprimanded by the Venture Scouts leader. He must have worked out it was me after the landlord of the pub complained.

My drinking has started slowly but soon I am drinking regularly. Mum has imposed a midnight curfew on me until I'm 18 years old. This isn't late enough for most of the events I go to, so I find a way round it. I sometimes stay at Simon's, my friend from Hunter and Maxwell. His parents give him plenty of leeway: he can come home any time he wants. Mum likes and trusts him so she never asks any questions.

We rarely go out into town but we don't need to. With most of the kids at my school coming from quite well-to-do parents, they all have parties when they reach sixteen or eighteen. Simon gets invited to most of them and I tag along. The parties are at venues that serve alcohol to underage kids. The favourite venue is a social club at the bottom of town. All the parties there are closed events so nobody can see what we get up to.

The only reason I drink is to get drunk, which is worrying because Mum is just the same. She never drinks socially, only at home to get wasted. I am drinking socially but I, too, want the same result, to enter the alternative universe I inhabit when I am drunk. I don't even like the taste of most drinks. Bitter, lager, Guinness and spirits are drinks I only touch if they're really cheap. I hate brandy because Mum drinks it. I like cider, sherry and liqueurs because they are sweet. But getting drunk is the name of the game and I soon discover a different drink that does exactly that: Gold Label barley wine – 10.9% alcohol.

Simon likes his drink even more than me, especially beer. Like most lads our age, we just want to get drunk. The constant flow of parties means that I have a pretty good social life. I do naughty things, such as doing runners from taxis. I get the driver to drop me off in a dead-end street close to home, usually next to a wall with a field on the other side. Then I hurdle the wall and run across the field. I'm a fit young lad and no taxi driver ever catches me.

* * *

One reason I do runners is because I genuinely don't have the money to pay. The only reason I can afford going out at all is because I still have a paper round. My previous job was a 'normal' morning paper round where I got paid £4 a week for getting up six days a week and working for an hour and a half each day. After I burgled the paper shop, I understandably got sacked.

My new paper round is different – a Sunday round operated like a business. I deliver the papers for three hours every Sunday morning, having bought the round from the previous owner for £60. For this, I get a patch and a client list of houses that buy a paper when I deliver to their door. I buy my papers from a tiny shop in Mystendyke only open on a Sunday and do this on a sale-or-return basis.

The prices are less than the cover price. The difference is my profit. At this time, the *News of the World* is 28p – I buy it for 20p. The *Sunday Times* is 50p – I pay 30p. The paper round is a gold mine. I am making £13–£15 a week for just three hours' work. The downside is I have to get up at 7.30 am to do the round when I may be out until the early hours the night before. But this is a small price to pay for such a lucrative job. I also discover that I have an entrepreneurial streak.

I like being my own boss, owning my own round, buying and selling and working out my profit and collecting monies due. I also see a chance to make more money than the previous owners. I know the two brothers who've sold me the round. I buy it in September and they say that at Christmas I'll get about £15 in tips. I think this is cool as it means I get extra money when I need it the most.

But when Christmas comes I try something different. I buy a pack of the cheapest Christmas cards I can find for £3, then handwrite a card to every single one of my 100 customers. When I deliver them with their paper, the effect is astonishing. Only two customers don't give me a Christmas tip. I end up with £85, a huge amount to me in 1986. I enjoy having made so much from the tips. More than that, I like having done it when the other two lads haven't. I feel like a mini-business man and revel in that feeling.

I see no particular evidence of any business flair in my immediate family, apart from Uncle Jim, Mum's older brother. I saw him when he came to Grandad's funeral and he turned up once, out of the blue, in my early teens. He had remarried and not even told Mum, his only sibling, let alone invited her or me and Reg to the wedding.

But around this time when I'm seventeen we visit him in Kent. As usual, when we go to visit relatives we stay at a campsite. This one is near his home and we spend time with him and his family.

They live in a beautiful house; run a nice car. They are living a life far removed from ours in Halifax. Jim is manager and I believe part owner of one of the largest slate quarries in Europe. We go there one day and it is vast. I am always interested in cars and vehicles and to see these huge earth-moving JCBs is just astonishing. It's obvious Jim is a serious businessman making a lot of money.

Jim is on his third wife, twenty years younger than him. They have two children together and he has four from two previous marriages. While we're there he spends almost no time with his wife and kids. We go to his house on several evenings and once we've finished eating the meal she's cooked for us, we all go to the pub, leaving his wife at home with the children. Jim then gets totally hammered and we don't leave until past closing time.

As I get to know him I realize that he can be a difficult man. There's a certain element of selfishness to his personality and he isn't averse to causing trouble. I don't realize though that by now, like Mum, he's also an alcoholic.

After that trip, I never see him alive again. Through self-neglect and self-abuse he has effectively ended his own life and dies shortly afterwards, without even reaching his fiftieth birthday.

* * *

My eighteenth birthday is 6 April 1986, just a few months before my A levels. I ask for money as a gift: Mum gives me £150 and Dad the same. Mum always saves – that's how she is able to buy a car with cash, to go on holiday every year and to have no loan or credit card. I still find it astonishing how she does it although, of course, I'm not privy to her financial circumstances.

I decide to spend the money on a holiday. Simon and three other lads have booked a coach trip to the South of France, staying on a campsite. Although I hate camping with a passion, this is different. The idea of two weeks in France, getting pissed and hopefully laid every night really appeals. Camping makes it possible because it's cheap. It would cost double staying in a hotel.

The trip is memorable but not always for the right reasons. I spend all my money on alcohol, eating just enough during the day to soak up what I'm going to drink in the evening. But no matter how much I drink, I never completely lose control and always remember what has happened the night before. Simon isn't so lucky.

Like Mum, he drinks excessively, then loses control and does truly crazy things which can end up badly. One night, he gets so drunk that he's completely out of control. Even though the rest of us have drunk a great deal too, we can tell he's heading for trouble.

One thing Simon wants to do when drunk is to fight and on this particular night he starts on us.

'Come on then, I'll fucking have you,' he shouts, not looking at any of us in particular.

We all back off so as not to antagonize him.

'Scared of me, are you, you soft bunch of wankers.'

As he moves forward, one of the other lads responds by hitting him straight in the face. Simon goes down like a sack of potatoes and starts bleeding badly from his eye. It's clear he's in trouble. As the only one who can speak French, I have to sort out a doctor. Eventually, one comes and I guide him through the maze of tents to ours. Simon is taken to hospital where he is told that he has nearly lost his sight in that eye. This completely changes the tone of the whole holiday. The trips to see Simon aren't much fun and are costing us too: we've paid £25 for the doctor and are paying train fares on top. Despite the fact that we are facing difficult circumstances I decide to phone Mum. She responds by sending me some money which astonishingly actually arrives a few days later at the camp site which is full of thousands of tents in the South of France.

Seeing Simon lose control when drunk reminds me so much of Mum. He doesn't seem to remember what he's done. When we speak to him about the eye incident, we lie to him at first about what has happened and he accepts it completely. This apparent drunken amnesia answers one burning question in my head. Up until this point, I have often wondered if Mum remembers what she does to me when drunk. If she doesn't, then I can accept it as part of her alcoholism. But if she can remember and is in control, this would mean that she knows she has been asking her son for sex when drunk. This is different altogether and would have changed the way I perceive her.

But while drunk, Simon takes on a complete character change, turning into a raging monster. He can't remember anything he did or said while in this highly charged state. I sincerely believe it's the same for Mum.

* * *

Back from holiday, it's time for my exam results. Mum takes me to school and waits outside. When I go in, everyone's standing around talking, mainly discussing whether they have enough for their first choice of university. I'm hoping I've done enough just to pass a few with decent grades.

When I get to the huge board where the results are collated, I scan down looking for my grades. My worst fears are confirmed: I have one bottom grade pass and nothing else. I won't be going to university.

As I get back to the car, Mum can see how unhappy I am and when I show her the results she bursts into tears. I can understand her being upset, but it ends up as another role-reversal situation. She should be strong for me, giving me moral support. Instead, I am having to do this for her, saying that everything's going to be fine.

With my apparently calm exterior she's looking to me for an alternative plan. But there is no Plan B. It's time to start looking for a job. I talk it through with her and she suggests nursing. Immediately, I discount it, considering it a job for women. After all, Mum trained to be a nurse. But the more I think about it, the more it appeals. I decide to apply to become a trainee and almost immediately I'm called in for an interview. I dress as smartly as I can and off I go.

I'm excited and nervous. I've got used to the idea of being a nurse and badly want the job. I like the idea of helping people and know there are lots of different kinds of nursing jobs. It's a career move I can expect to do for a long time. After all, they are always going to need nurses. I go to the nursing head office and wait with a few other people who look as nervous as me. Eventually, it's my turn and I'm ushered into the office. I'm met by a lady who has real presence – she has authority and looks in complete control.

'Please sit down, Mr Thomas,' she says briskly.

I sit down, feverishly trying to think of the answers I've prepared.

She looks across the table at me and gets straight to the point. 'I have looked at your application form and I'm sorry to say we can't accept you as a trainee nurse.'

I feel like I've been hit by a lightning bolt. 'But why?' I ask, almost choking on my own words.

'Because you have a criminal record,' she replies.

She looks at me as if to say: it should be obvious. I remembered putting it down on my application form as it had been a legal requirement: the conditional discharge has only just expired but I still have to declare it for a fixed period afterwards. But I never thought it would deny me a chance to be a nurse. As it was two years ago I've forgotten all about it. I go home feeling numb. I've been out of trouble for two years without the thought of burglary even entering my mind, let alone doing it. It's another example of how my period of criminal activity is going to affect me for a long time.

This rejection hits me hard. I don't want it to happen again so I do a bit of research. I discover that some occupations would be able to legally force me to declare my conviction, no matter how far into the future I apply. One example is the police force. If I want to apply to join the police even in twenty years' time, I'd still have to declare my record. But there's some good news. Under the Rehabilitation of Offenders Act 1974, my conviction will be considered a 'spent' conviction six months after the conditional discharge expires. Almost all jobs adhere to this Act and so I just need to wait until that time is up and I won't have to declare it. Even armed with this new information I still feel disappointed and angry at myself. I'm also without a job which I badly need so I start looking round.

I get interviews for two jobs and am offered both of them. The one I take is working for Halifax First, a car-insurance company. Being as risk averse as ever, Mum pushes me into the job, saying how important it is to have a job with security and a future.

I hate it from the first day — every single second. For a start, I'm working in an office where there are only four men and twenty women. I don't have the social skills to deal with women and struggled to know what to say or do. I hate the confines of an office and the fact that it's nine to five. And I hate doing a job where I'm only getting £70 a week. It isn't enough money. I want a higher wage not because I want to buy clothes or a car or go out every night, but because I want to leave home.

I have finally realized that Mum's never going to change and my patience has run out. I have endured her drinking problem for most of my eighteen years. Between them, Reg and Mum have punched, kicked and thrown things at me, abusing their position in the worst possible way with his savage beatings and her constant demands to have sex with me. It's time to leave home. I've had enough.

PART 3

Another Kind of Memory

13

Into the Fire

My escape comes in the form of a girl from Blackholme called Janice. She's older than me with always perfectly coiffeured big hair, as befits her job as a hairdresser. We consider buying a house but have little money so we decide to rent. I like Janice a lot but I don't love her. I just want to get away from Mum and would go anywhere to do so. Stupidly, we move into a house which is £180 a month in rent. Janice is only on £70 a week too so it takes one of our monthly wages just to pay for food, rent and bills. I get in touch with Dad and ask him for financial assistance: he sends me a set of cutlery through the post – all the way from America.

Janice and I struggle and after six months decide we can't afford to live there any longer. She moves back in with her grandad and I tell Mum I'll be moving back in with her. She's over the moon; I most definitely am not. As the moving date approaches I start to panic. I really don't want to go back home. I am still going up every Sunday for the family roast dinner and I know her drinking is as bad as ever. I can't bear the thought of returning to that hellhole.

I look in the paper for some cheap accommodation and find a bedsit. I'm delighted as it means I don't have to move back home. My wage is still low but I don't care. Although basic, the bedsit is clean and the location perfect – within walking distance of both work and Halifax town centre, for my shopping and the like, which means no travel costs. I can also walk into Halifax for my nights out.

* * *

Over the next eight years, going out is the single most important thing in my life.

I like going out on my own but having a drinking buddy is much better and that person is Tim. I met him at Hunter and Maxwell school and we used to get the bus home together. He was quite a shy lad then, but underneath I think he had his own problems. Maybe because of this we've gravitated towards each other. When I begin working at Halifax First, we keep in touch. I tell him he should pack his schooling in and come and work there. He does, and from that moment on we become inseparable.

We go out together in town, doing it as cheaply as possible. We go into clubs at 9.30 pm before you have to pay. I even steal people's drinks. I don't care what the drink is. If it's free, I drink it. I even steal half-drunk drinks and put them all in one pint pot. I know this is disgusting but it's funny. I pride myself on my thriftiness: I can go out into Halifax, get drunk, stay out until three, walk home and not spend a single penny.

The thrill of going out is electrifying. I love the dance music and the energy of pubs and clubs. It's like landing on a different planet where normal rules don't apply. I can get away with behaviour otherwise considered unacceptable. I enjoy the fact that alcohol removes my inhibitions. I don't like the quiet evenings in my bedsit though. It isn't that I mind my own company but I get bored easily. So I start drinking at home. It isn't a serious attempt to block things out, more to make the evening go more quickly.

My alcohol of choice is the coffee liqueur, Tia Maria. Mixed with Coca-Cola I can easily drink a full bottle in one evening. I won't drink every evening but it becomes more frequent. Despite twenty years of dealing with Mum's alcohol dependency, I'm developing the same habit. But there's one crucial problem which is to destroy my descent into alcoholism: I can't afford it. My disposable income is only £180 a month; Tia Maria is £10 a bottle. I'm not eating much and substituting Tia Maria for food. Even so I simply can't make my money stretch that far. So I stop drinking at home. This is an important landmark: I don't want to go the same way as Mum.

Work is increasingly painful. My output is monitored, as is everyone's. I'm doing as much as anyone else in the office but getting into the most trouble. It's mind-numbingly boring and I can work quickly. I can do a full day's processing in half a day and spend the rest of the time talking to people and wandering around the office. The whole thing's driving me crazy.

I wanted to work in an office where I could work normal hours, wear a nice suit and not get my hands dirty, but the office has turned into a prison. So I decide to go for another job. I buy all the local papers and the *Yorkshire Post* on job night. I don't think the YP will have anything suitable as they advertise jobs all over the county. I have no car and don't want to buy one unless the wage is significantly higher, which is unlikely as I have no qualifications. But I buy it anyway.

Then one week, as I'm looking through the ads, my prayers are answered with a tiny advertisement – a recruitment ad to join the Fire Service.

* * *

I'm immediately interested but not for the usual reasons. Most guys want to become firefighters because they like the perceived glamour – with lots of women fancying them. But I like the idea because the starting wage is double what I'm on at Halifax First and I don't need any specific qualifications.

The failure rate for getting into the Fire Service is extremely high: only one in 40 get through the selection process which makes me think twice about applying. But the more I think about it, the more I fancy it. For a start, it's about as far away from my current job as it could possibly be. It involves shifts and working weekends. I will be using my hands which I've never done before. I will be under immense pressure to perform, both as a recruit and as an operational firefighter.

More than anything, I start to imagine how it would make me feel to tell people I'm a firefighter and immediately have a growing sense of self-esteem. People will look up to me. Very soon it goes from being desirable to essential for me to get into the Fire Service. I just have to get in. I know it will be hard and I'll need some luck but I'm really going to give it a try. I apply in February and over the following nine months go through the selection process.

It's nerve wracking. On the day of the physical 24 guys start, but through the day, officers keep coming in and calling out numbers. If you have that number you go off with the officer and will never be seen again. Even when the numbers are getting whittled down, we're told that only six will make it to training school – just 25% of those who turned up at 8 am. But it's also deeply stimulating and rewarding. As I go from one level to the next, my confidence and self-belief increase. When they eventually offer me the job, I'm beyond words.

The day I go into Halifax First to tell them I'm leaving is the best day of my life. I've worked so hard to get into the Fire Service and beaten off thousands of other guys to get one of the few coveted places at training school. At last I'm going to be doing something worthwhile with my life. It may even make things better for Mum. She's delighted for me, even though she's concerned about the obvious dangerous situations that firefighters go into, but she thinks it great that I have a secure job with a long career.

She can also take credit for one thing: I'm told later that one of the reasons I've got to the first level of selection and a chance to do the written tests is because I have studied at A level. Every officer from the Chief Fire Officer down has to start at the bottom of the ladder and work his way up, but the vast majority who join the Fire Service are blue-collar workers who've come from a manually skilled occupation such as plumbing, building or truck driving.

So when they select people to join the service they're always on the lookout for people who have studied at a higher level than just to the age of 16. These individuals are needed as they're more likely to pass the difficult exams required to get to a senior position in the Fire Service. Even though I have only passed one A level, the fact that I have gone into the sixth form potentially puts me in that category. Mum pushed me to go into the sixth form and I'll always be grateful to her for that.

Joining the Fire Service is to be a life-changing experience. As the saying goes, I join as a boy and it turns me into a man. I learn so much about people, challenges, pressure – and life itself. I become skilled in things I never thought I'd ever be able to do. But there's one thing that puzzles me.

The Fire Service has let me in with a criminal record. I have studied the application form and decided I don't need to declare it. But I will come to understand that I can't just airbrush away my life history as easily as ignoring a question on a sheet.

Eventually, the Service find out about my juvenile criminal conviction after I have joined, which creates a very big problem that is going to threaten my whole future.

* * *

I leave Halifax First in December 1988. It wasn't a bad place to work. It just wasn't for me. It was full of people on low wages doing boring jobs. They wanted automatons and that isn't me. They have no idea how to get the best out of me or stretch me. But I don't care. I'm going to a job that will stretch me to my limits.

In January 1989 I set off from my bedsit to begin my 14 weeks' training at West Yorkshire Fire Service training centre, Birkenshaw, Bradford. It's a daunting but exciting prospect. I am confident that I can do this job, having succeeded where 97.5% of applicants have failed. They chose me because they thought I could do the job. In reality I have no idea what to expect. I'm an office boy who's never worked with his hands and who's never had a father figure in his life. This, combined with the fact that I'm only 20, means that I struggle from the moment I start in the Fire Service.

The manual side is the hardest aspect of the job. Using hose couplings and portable pumps is completely alien to me. Even using the basic toolkit is difficult. I can barely remember the different names, let alone how to use them. Lads who are tradesmen like plumbers and electricians take to it like a duck to water and I marvel at their natural ability to use machinery.

I struggle with the constant shouting and discipline. It's not that I don't want to do as I'm told. I may have demonstrated a rebellious streak in the past but I have grown up since then. This is definitely not the time or place to start throwing my weight about with other students and instructors. I know how to keep my mouth shut but whenever I do something wrong, an instructor comes and bawls straight into my ear at the top of his voice, which is completely counter-productive. It makes me more nervous than ever and I lose my focus. I assume they are putting us under pressure because that's how it is in a fire situation.

The attention to detail is exhausting too, especially with cleaning and uniforms. We have four different uniforms – work clothes, fire kit, dress uniform and PE kit. They have to be immaculate at all times. Even the work clothes – dungarees and sweatshirt – have to have creases perfectly ironed down the front. I can't see the point but on a Monday morning we have to parade for the Commandant in our work clothes and we're in trouble if everything isn't immaculate. Because of this parade and the fact that I have no car, I have to iron my work clothes at home then carry them on the bus all the way from Halifax to Bradford, which means getting up at 5 am.

The worst bit is cleaning the shoes. In typical service style, polishing shoes to a bright shine isn't enough. We have to 'bull' them, cleaning the toes with cotton wool dipped in water and endlessly going around in tiny circles building up the layers until eventually achieving a bright shine. The guys who've been in the Armed Forces know what they're doing but I don't. I never get them to where I want them to be and sweat buckets at the two parades we do every week in case they aren't good enough.

But struggling with the work, discipline and cleaning is nothing compared with my inability to deal with banter between the lads. Working in an office, the people around me were relatively mild-mannered and easy-going. There was no bad language or rude jokes, no sexual innuendo or shouting.

Training School is the exact opposite. Everyone is quick to take the mickey out of each other and sometimes it's personal. It takes a thick skin to deal with that and I don't have it. I'm still only 20 when the average age on my course is 25. Some guys have been working for the last fifteen years. I'm wet behind the ears and struggle with the laddish behaviour. My reluctance to get stuck into the others, combined with my young age, mean that I'm easy prey to the mouthy older recruits. I'm not bullied but receive more than my fair share of stick.

As is the way in the Fire Service, nicknames are popular. After we've been at training school for a few weeks, it becomes obvious I'm not going to win Top Recruit. I'm struggling on all fronts.

'Here, Thomas,' one lad shouts across a room full of recruits.

'What?'

'I've got a nickname for you.'

I know it isn't going to be a nice one, but have to ask anyway. 'Oh yeah, what's that then?' I try to look as if I didn't care.

'Thrombo,' he replies. 'It stands for thrombosis, as in a slow-moving clot.'

Everyone roars with laughter. I suppose if it were about anyone else I would laugh too.

'Ha, ha, very funny,' I say, going bright red. I'm learning that getting on in the Fire Service is about survival of the fittest and standing your ground. I'm never going to be the best recruit firefighter in the world but I do enjoy it. I'm not the quickest learner either, but I pick up enough to get me through to the end of the course.

As I go through my training I have many issues but it never occurs to me to leave. The reason for this is the weekend. When I go out on a Saturday night I see people I know who've previously known me as David the Office Worker. But now I'm David the Firefighter. They look at me differently, with deference and respect. They know what it means to be a firefighter and how hard it is to get in.

Once the 14 weeks are up, I have my Passing Out Parade – the recruits' chance to show off to our invited guests. My guests are Mum, Reg and Janice, who I've now been seeing for two years. I feel very proud that I've reached this milestone. It wasn't guaranteed that I'd end up passing out and I can feel my chest swell as we do our last-ever parade. I have done something significant in my life and that feels amazing.

* * *

My increased confidence has transferred into other areas. I've started lifting weights. I love going to the gym and the idea of being muscular and in great shape. I want that look and am prepared to work for it. My new-found work ethic installed in me at Training School comes to the fore in the gym. I go regularly and soon start putting on some quality muscle. I change my diet and am eating chicken, rice, tuna and protein drinks.

I'm turning into a gym monster and love it. The body-building lifestyle suits me because of my shifts on the fire station and it fits in with going out. But even though I'm training hard and love the way my body is changing, I never take steroids. I see plenty of people who do and know I can get my hands on them if I want to.

I never even think seriously about taking steroids.

The decision isn't a moral one. I fully understood why some lads take the stuff. They train hard and lead a life most people never understand. They want to maximize their dedication to their sport and I never condemn that. But I just don't fancy it for myself. There are incidents in the gym where someone ends up in hospital or has a bad batch of gear. I also know I have an addictive character. If I started taking steroids, enough would never be enough. I would take ever stronger drugs to get as big as I possibly can. It's a road I don't want to go down.

I am now in a position I have never been in before, feeling confident and my self-esteem is at an all-time high. I have a decent wage coming in, which means I can do what I want. I move to a different bedsit in the same house, a small increase in rent but it's on the ground floor which I prefer.

Going out on a weekend is important to me so I make a conscious decision to spend all my money doing just that. Once I go out, I drink to extreme, though never to the point where I'm completely out of control. I never go to a local pub either. Sitting on the end of a bar chatting to other locals about the weather never appeals to me. I only want to go out into town and hit a nightclub.

I learn that how I dress is important. Girls like a guy who's smartly dressed and well groomed. I spend money on buying good clothes and wear a two-piece suit with shirt and tie when I go out. I look good, am in great physical shape and alcohol loosens my tongue. I soon learn to say what a woman wants to hear. The fact that I am telling them I'm a firefighter is a distinct bonus.

I'm not the best-looking lad in the world but when I go out I have the confidence to talk to women, which has a huge, positive effect on my life, although it's later to cause me major problems.

* * *

I am having less contact with Mum. I phone her mid-week to organize going up on a weekend for the Sunday roast dinner. I see her on Sunday for the meal. She rarely calls round to the bedsit and I have no phone or mobile so I'm not contactable. That's how I want it. When I do go, Reg tells me about Mum's drinking. It's getting worse but I don't know what to do about it and don't even care as much about it now. I'm living a fun life, independent of Mum and don't want her spoiling it.

I now have a reckless attitude to life where I'm up for anything and sod the consequences. I've spent many years learning how to compartmentalize my feelings because when Mum's sober what happens when she's drunk never gets mentioned and I never tell anyone. I think this has caused me to cut off my feelings when my relationships finish. I am living completely in the moment and with my addictive personality that isn't necessarily a good thing.

* * *

My probationary period as a firefighter is rocky. I thought that landing on station from training school would make everything alright, but it doesn't. I find station life very different to the one I've left at Training School. Discipline is lax and some members of the Watch, particularly the old-timers, dress scruffily. But I like the lifestyle.

The manual aspect of the job is still causing me huge problems. I understand the mechanics of how things work but don't have the natural knack of applying it in the field. I make simple mistakes and all this does is deplete my confidence even further: I live two lives as a fireman. When talking to people away from the Fire Service I big it up as people are always dead impressed when I tell them I'm a fireman. But on station I struggle and the confidence I had when I first started slowly depletes with each error.

The situation is made a thousand times worse by the officer in charge of my shift. He doesn't like many people on the shift but he particularly dislikes probationers, especially ones that aren't much good like me. I feel he does nothing to help me along and sometimes goes out of his way to show me up. I start to lose confidence in myself and my ability.

Twelve months after I've gone on station he recommends my dismissal from the Service. I am stunned. I have worked hard to get where I am and I'm now used to being a firefighter. I even like the shifts as they allow me to go the gym during the day and go out clubbing on a night. I don't want to lose my job. His recommendation brings a senior officer down to the station to see me for an interview in the Station Office. This officer is known for being a pitbull and a bully who treats all firefighters with disdain. It isn't going to be fun.

'Your Station Officer recommends you be dismissed from the Fire Service,' he says, looking at me as if I were dirt.

'Yes, sir, I know. But can I just say—'

'No, you can't. Your Station Officer is highly experienced and has trained up many probationers. I think we can safely say he knows best.'

This is going even worse than I'd feared. I'm hoping I'll get the chance to give my side to a neutral observer. No such luck.

'But, sir, I'd like to say—'

'You will go on monthly reports. The first time you get a bad one, you will be dismissed. You may leave.' He doesn't even look up at me.

I go home feeling very unhappy and sorry for myself. There's no way that my Station Officer will give me a good report. I have a month left and that's the end of my Fire Service career. I start looking for jobs in the paper. I even contemplate ringing Halifax First to see if they have any vacancies.

Then I get angry. I decide to fight him to keep my job. The next time I go into work, I ask my Station Commander if I can speak to him. We go into his office.

'Boss, I'd like to transfer shift.'

This is a big request and not one that will be granted lightly. It means only one thing – that I'm not happy with my Station Officer. I also know that it could backfire on me. If my request isn't granted, my Station Officer will definitely give me a bad report next month and I'll be out. He'll see it as an attack on his integrity. So it's an all or nothing strategy.

'I don't think that's going to happen, David,' he says.

I feel sick when he says this but decide to pursue it anyway. 'Look, boss, I'm on monthly reports and we know why that is. He doesn't like me and he wants to have me kicked out. I know I haven't been the best probationer but I should get another chance with a different boss.'

He looks thoughtful so I press it home. 'There's a vacancy on Green Watch. I could go over there. If I'm going to get sacked, at least let me see if I can do better under someone different.'

He thinks about it for a second before replying, 'Well, I promise you that I will phone Headquarters and ask the DO. If he says yes, then you can.'

My heart sinks. The DO he mentions is the one who interviewed me and put me on report in the first place. I have a few anxious hours and then receive the news I've been praying for: I get my move.

After that, things immediately improve. The guy in charge of my new shift, Green Watch, is my old Sub

Officer and he's great, helping me through my probation. The probationary period is extended by three months but I make it through. I'm now a permanent operational firefighter. No-one can take that away from me.

Things are a little easier now that I've passed my probation, so I decide to sit my promotion exams. I have never struggled with the written and academic side of the Fire Service. After all, with the vast majority of applicants being working-class tradesmen they couldn't make the tests too hard or everyone would fail. Having studied at A level, I don't find the exams hard. I study for promotion, but then fail the written exams badly. I'm really upset and decide to have a word with an officer about it.

'Look, son,' he says, 'you're obviously not good enough to pass. Forget the idea of promotion.'

It's a sweeping statement based on no knowledge whatsoever and gives me no encouragement to try again. Of course, I assume he knows best so I take his advice and leave the thought of promotion well alone. But I will soon prove him wrong in spectacular fashion.

14

Heartbreaker

After Dad emigrated to America when I was eleven his
input into my life had been marginal to say the least. He
sent the occasional letter, and phone calls were limited to
twice a year at Christmas and on my birthday. He came
over in 1982 but I only saw him for a short while. When I
was sixteen and got in trouble with the police, he came
over to the UK. It was fantastic to see him. But even
though he was here for a while, I only saw him for one day.
That was typical of Dad. He hadn't seen me in several
years and then thought that one day was sufficient.

While over here, he had tried to have a father–son chat
about my troubles but it came across all wrong. He didn't
have the interpersonal skills to have any impact on me and
so the conversation was uneasy for both of us. But I am
now in my early twenties and feel that maybe I can make a
connection from this side.

I begin writing letters to him regularly. I want him to
be proud of me and the fact that I'm now a firefighter. I
tell him about my weight training too. I make the letters
personal and chatty. It's my way of reaching out to him
and I desperately want him to reach back too. But it isn't

to be. I have some letters back but they're always brief and detached. He talks about the weather or work he's done on his house. That isn't what I'm looking for. He finds it difficult to offer compliments. I feel I have achieved a big success in my life by becoming a firefighter, especially when I consider the mess I have been in just a few short years before. I'm hoping there might be some real recognition of this. But not so.

I conclude that he loves me but that he doesn't care. Or at least, he doesn't put that care into action. To do this, you need to actively show sympathy, compassion, interest and spend time with someone, either face to face or on the phone. You need to share their triumphs and sorrows. Dad demonstrates none of these traits to me. It is clear that I don't enter his thoughts often enough for him to make that kind of effort. I give up writing to him as it is too upsetting.

Despite this, in 1991 I stay in his house in Richmond, Virginia, spending nearly a month with him and Maureen. The trip is a great success overall. I go in October and have wonderful weather. It's the first time in America for me and I love it. Dad and Maureen make me feel welcome and give me complete freedom: he even has a spare car so I can get around. Their house is on a 22-acre patch of land. It's fantastic to wake up in the morning and go out into the meadow and woodland.

I've spent a little time with Maureen previously and spoken to her on the phone. She's a fantastic woman, the complete opposite of my father – chatty, funny and personal. I instantly take a huge liking to her and follow her around like a puppy dog.

* * *

During our trip Dad takes a week off and we go on the road. We have a good time but it seems to highlight the difference between us. He has a lot of patience though and does pretty much what I want to do. Staying overnight in Gatlinburg, Tennessee, we go out in the evening and get pretty drunk. Dad returns to the motel before me and says to meet him at 9 am next morning.

Once he's gone I get up to my usual tricks. I look for some women I can chat up and soon get talking to one. She's plain, blonde, and quite shy, and I end up going back to her motel and staying there for the night. In the morning I wake up late and shoot out of bed and back to my motel. As I turn the corner to my room, Dad's sitting on the balcony.

'Hiya, Dad,' I say, a little put out that he's seen me.

He looks me over with his usual deadpan expression. 'Good morning, David,' he replies.

I dash in and get my stuff together. We get in the car and set off for Nashville. We've been going about an hour when Dad decides to ask a question.

'David, were you just coming in this morning when I saw you?'

'Yes, Dad, I was.'

He never says another word. I can only guess what he's thinking, but he just can't bring himself to say anything about it.

There are many positive things about spending time with Dad on that trip. He has a wicked sense of humour.

'Why is Huddersfield the home of the mucky cow?'

'I don't know, Dad.'

'Because she likes having her udders feeled.'

He delivers this without so much as a flicker in his face, as if telling a very straight story. He'd make a great poker player.

Dad looks better to me now than he did when he was younger. For one thing, his hair, though thinner and starting to grey, is slightly longer and he has a moustache as well as a beard so it looks much more natural than the thick black beard he used to wear when I was a child, which looked like it was stuck to his chin with glue.

Dad also shows me he can put himself out when he chooses to. Far more important, we make a connection, albeit a small one. I hope for bigger things between us after the trip is over. Maureen senses this and puts it into a more realistic perspective for me. One day, she and I go shopping. I mention that we've had a good road trip and that I feel that Dad and I have made a connection.

'I saw the letters you wrote to your Dad,' she says, 'and I felt for you. I could see you were reaching out to him.' She looks me in the eye and intensifies her stare. 'But you'll never get what you're looking for. It's just not there.'

She goes on to explain why. Dad has just enough ability to have one full relationship and that's with her. It sounds like she's being possessive but she really isn't. I know she's absolutely right. Maureen can see things with crystal clarity and she puts it across to me in a kind and succinct way.

I go home from the trip with that thought in my head and she's right. Back in the UK, the usual contact resumes: I may have spent quality time with him in the US but in reality, nothing has changed.

* * *

My relationship with his mother, my grandmother has taken a turn for the worse. I have grown up loving and appreciating her for her quirks and eccentricities. She is a funny woman with a dry sense of humour, something Dad has inherited. She's good company and intelligent, able to put a different angle on things. She has been caring, affectionate and soft, the same as Mum could be but without all the drunken rage that comes with it. It's important for me to keep in touch with her and I make the effort to visit her on a regular basis. Unfortunately, this just isn't enough.

When I'm 23, I go to see her on Mother's Day. I'll also be seeing Mum but think it would be nice to visit Grandma first. I buy some flowers and take the bus to her house. What follows is extraordinary, even for her. I go up to the front door as I always do and knock on the door. I don't have Grandma's phone number as she won't give it to me but I've told her on a previous visit that I will be coming today. There's no reply to my knock so I knock again. Still no reply.

'Hiya, Grandma,' I shout from the outside, 'it's me, David.'

Nothing. I put my head down and open the letterbox. Immediately there's some movement. Grandma has been on the other side of the door listening to me and as I open the letterbox, she scurries into the living room.

'Hiya Grandma,' I speak through the letterbox, 'it's me, David. I've brought you some flowers.'

No reply. I stand up. As I do, I look to my left. She has a mirror in her window that allows her to see who's at the front door. I'm now watching her watching me. Very surreal. I move to the window. As I get there, I look inside and am taken by surprise. She's on the other side of the window looking straight at me, just a few feet away. She stares at me for a second and before I can wave or smile or coax her into letting me in, she runs off upstairs. I wait a few more minutes then realize she isn't going to let me in. I lay the flowers down and go up to Mum's house with some more flowers.

I try several more times to get into Grandma's house but every time this ends in failure. Eventually, I give up altogether. I have no idea why she's never wanted to see me again. I have done nothing wrong or said anything to upset her. Only she knows the answer. But I shouldn't be so surprised. Some years earlier she disowned her own sister in similar fashion.

* * *

By now I have been through several relationships after breaking up with Janice. I have spent most of my teenage years feeling rejected by girls. But these days I'm able to pick them up at will and I'm making the most of it. I have become addicted to picking up girls and just want to have sex with as many women as I can. Cheating, lying, being unfaithful come naturally to me in the endless pursuit of the next girl. Once I'm drunk I'll hit on any woman, regardless of looks, age or marital state. I don't care. I'll tell her what she wants to hear until we've had sex. Then I make up some excuse about an ex-girlfriend getting pregnant and we finish.

I know it's not making me happy but even if I wanted to, which I don't at this point, I can't seem to escape this cycle. The unhappier I am, the more I try to block it out by getting drunk and finding yet another girl. Deep down, I may be aware that I'm starting to feel as bad about myself as I have always imagined my mother did about herself. But I won't allow myself to think about it.

My pickup venue is a Halifax nightclub called the Acapulco, a great club with fantastic dance tunes and full of loose women. There's a liberal approach to sex from both sides in the Acca. Week after week I go in and pull women. I sleep with one girl one week, her sister the next. However they come, I'm not bothered. In the Acca, my sole mission is to go home with a woman. If I go home alone, the night's a failure. It may have been brilliant in every other respect but it's all about the women. I don't even have to be drunk or on a night out. I'm always on the lookout for women wherever I am. Because of my shift pattern, I have a lot of spare time so I'll wander into town and chat to girls who are hanging around doing nothing. All these liaisons end with sex at my place.

I am dimly aware that in some way I am replicating my mother's behaviour towards me throughout my childhood – that I'm doing to these women what Mum did to me – but I can't stop myself and I don't want to stop myself. I am way out of control at this stage in my life for those kinds of moral restraints.

My desire for constant sex often makes things complicated. Several times I'm in bed with one girl at 3 am when another knocks on my window. I then say it's an ex-girlfriend and that she's unstable and there could be trouble. The girl in bed with me leaves by the back door while the other one comes in the front. My sex life also interferes with my work. Sometimes, I stay out so late that I get home in the early hours with only enough time left for me to have a shower and go to work. I do my day shift then go out and do it all again the following night.

My life is running on automatic, like the springs in a piece of clockwork that have been wound up too tight for too long and can only uncoil mechanically. I am now devoid of any kind of feeling for the women I have sex with, just as I myself was simply an object, a human toy, for my mother, all those long, dark, endless nights of my childhood.

I truly believe at this time that I can sleep all I want once I'm dead. My approach to going out is: drink as much as you can; sleep with as many women as you can. I don't look for trouble when I go out. If someone walks into me I always apologize before they turn round, even though it isn't my fault. If I spill a guy's drink I immediately buy him another.

I love it all. I love the control that having a good job with a decent wage gives me. I enjoy the confidence boost I get when women sleep with me. I like the fact that I don't have to rely on Mum for anything and that she's playing a peripheral part in my life. But although it's peripheral, she's still always there.

* * *

I see her every Sunday for the family meal. On most occasions Mum is fine. But sometimes she drinks and when she does, it causes monumental rows and problems. She wanders all over the house, half naked. She is abusive, shouting obscenities at us. She never eats when drunk so Reg and I will sit and eat, while she constantly interrupts the meal.

By now Reg is actually talking to me about her drinking. He bears the brunt of what she fancies dishing out when she's drunk as he's now the only one living with her. He tells me that she's hitting him, but he doesn't need to tell me this: I can see the bruises all over the back of his hands where he's been putting them up to defend himself.

The sad irony of course is that when I was a boy, Reg was the one handing out the beatings to me while Mum said nothing, although she knew about it. Now Reg is receiving the same treatment from her. He's deeply upset by it all and he can't control it. He's 83 years old and too physically infirm to deal with her. He should be relaxing, enjoying his twilight years, not having to fend off his drunken, abusive wife. I feel I can't let this go.

This is a dangerous situation. I know how bad she can get. I remember how forceful she was when she wanted me to play with her and tried to mount me and rape me while I was half asleep. I remember the punches in the face, the kicks to the body and the black eyes, and I instinctively know that if she's half as bad with Reg as she's been with me, then real trouble is on the way. She could easily wake up and find Reg dead in the house some-where. So I decide that drastic action is required. I speak to Reg first and tell him my plan. He must leave the house and move to a location she doesn't know about. Then I'll go back to Mum and tell her she must address her alco-holism or Reg won't return.

Reg immediately says yes. He's so worn out with the sleepless nights and violence he would agree to anything. He just wants it to stop. I phone a local care home and ask if he can be accommodated, either temporarily or perma-nently. They know Reg and say they would be glad to take him. Then I phone Social Services and ask about drying-out clinics for Mum to go into. She's been in one before so I'm hoping that this might not be too much of a shock to her. Once it's all in place, I put the plan into action.

I tell Mum I'm taking Reg somewhere. She swallows it and off I go to the care home with him. It's only about four miles from where Mum lives but it's not a place she would naturally guess he would be. He settles into his room and I make sure he's comfortable before I leave him.

'I'll see you tomorrow,' I say to him.

'Ay, lad, alright,' he replies.

It isn't his style to say thank you but I know he's grateful that I'm doing this.

I'm not looking forward to speaking to her and have no idea what her response is going to be. I pass the house and see her looking out. She can see Reg isn't with me. As I enter the dining room she's sitting at the table looking pensive.

'Where's Reg?' she asks quietly, as if she already knows the answer but has to ask anyway.

'I've taken him somewhere safe,' I reply calmly. I know Mum might get hysterical at this news. 'He asked me to do it,' I continue, 'as he feels at risk with your drinking the way it's been recently. You must have seen the bruises on his hands that you've caused when you're drunk.'

She sits there, completely impassive. She's not going to admit to anything.

'So what now?' she says, still calm.

This is going much better than I had expected. At the very least, I had assumed she'd start shouting and bawling about my having overstepped the mark and demanding to know where Reg is. But there's none of that.

'Well, we're hoping you'd consider going into a treatment centre. We want you to get off the drink.'

She continues to look down into her hands and after a few moments she looks up. 'OK then. Where am I going?' she asks.

Oh ... My ... God!

I can't believe it. After all these years, I have managed to do something which might finally make Mum face up to the consequences of her actions.

This is a pivotal moment in my life. I have seen her systematically destroying herself and everything around her over a twenty-year period and because of a proactive step by me she will now be addressing the cause of all this pain. She packs a bag for herself and off she goes to the clinic. It isn't local and it's residential. I think this is for the best. That way, she can focus on her treatment completely.

I go back to see Reg the following day and tell him the good news. He's delighted, wanting her to stop drinking as much as me. Over the following few weeks Mum stays at the drying-out clinic, receiving treatment for her alcoholism. Reg stays at the care home and is well looked after by everyone there. I visit him every couple of days and spend time with him.

The minimum length of time for her treatment is five weeks. Bang on five weeks she phones to say she's coming home. I'm there to meet her.

'How did it go?' I ask anxiously. This is a very nervous moment for me. It's so important that this treatment works.

'Very well,' she smiles back.

I smile too. The wave of relief washing over me is overwhelming. I can feel a huge release as all the years of pain and anger started seeping out of my body. It's better than winning the pools.

I arrange to go and see Reg and have a chat with him about what he wants to do. I find him in his chair in the lounge.

'Hiya Reg, how's it going?'

'Ay, I'm alright lad,' he replies, looking pleased to see me. 'How's Carol?'

'Well, there's good news. She's back home now and she says the treatment worked very well.'

'That's good.' He looks as pleased and relieved as I was when I first heard the news.

'But remember, Reg, you don't have to go back to the house if you don't want to. We've been here before and you know it's not worked.'

Reg looks thoughtful as if contemplating this.

'You may want to stop here for a few more weeks, Reg, until I can check out Mum and make sure she's off the drink.'

He looks up and it's obvious what his decision is. 'I want to go home. Sort my things out and take me back.'

'Of course.'

I take Reg home to Mum and they have a tearful reunion. It's clear that despite a relationship which is incomprehensible to almost all who know them they have a rock-solid marriage and nothing is going to come between them.

But although I should have known by now, I little suspect what is just around the corner.

* * *

Throughout my schooling years I never had much confidence in my academic ability because of my poor exam results. Mum may have played a part in this. Despite everything that was happening at that time between us personally, she had always taken an active interest in my schooling and would push me to do my homework. But she did hold one simple belief: whatever intelligence you're born with, you're stuck with it.

At this point in my life I've come to accept this fatalistic view of myself. I remember when at the age of eleven I took Sally to see *Superman* and fantasized that I could be super-fit and super-intelligent with an amazing memory. I may have improved my physique and put on muscles, but I'm never going to improve myself in the brains department. I'm just not very good at remembering things, and that's been reflected in my poor academic performance, especially when it comes to taking exams – and there's no reason why that should change.

Like Mum says, I'm stuck with it.

I think it occurs to me though that maybe Mum's fatalistic attitude is why she's struggled with giving up the drink. When Reg temporarily went into the car home, she went into the drying-out clinic and came out five weeks later telling us she was fine. In fact, the opposite was the case. She left the clinic thinking she wasn't as bad as other people. She'd sat in group sessions and when she heard what the others had done, she immediately felt she was in the wrong place. She deluded herself into thinking that her drinking was less serious than everyone believed. Of course her problem was that she never remembered what she did when she was drunk. If she had, maybe she would have worked harder in the clinic. I could certainly have given her a different angle on her drinking.

In just a few weeks she's drinking again. But each time she returns to the bottle, she's worse than before. The problem of her phone abuse hasn't bothered me personally up until now because there was no phone in the bedsits I lived in and I had no mobile. I liked it that way. But by now I'm living in a house with a phone and Mum has access to me 24/7. When I first move in, she phones regularly to chat, but soon she's phoning all the time, often drunk. She also phones the fire station. Because she's drunk she can't remember what times I'm working. It's pot luck whether I'm on station, and often I'm not. She'll talk to whoever's there, telling them all kinds of personal information about me. When I turn up at work someone will make a snide comment about Mum having phoned on my days off and what she's said. When I mention it to her she just swats the question away. This is starting to seriously cheese me off.

I'm getting calls from Reg too. He regularly phones when Mum's drunk wanting me to go up and sort her out. With this kind of request, I'm torn. On the one hand I want to make sure she's OK. All those years of looking after her as a child and teenager have left me with that habitual desire. But I know if I go up, I could be there for hours, way past midnight, trying to calm her down. When Reg phones, I have to make a judgement call. Sometimes I go but if I think the situation isn't too serious, I won't go. But occasionally when he phones it's much more serious than just her getting drunk. One incident is particularly scary.

I'm getting ready to go out to a Christmas do when Reg phones, saying there's been a small fire at the house and could I go up. A small fire with Mum could mean anything and as a firefighter I know that what seems a harmless situation with a fire can quickly develop into something much larger. If it did, it could be very dangerous with Reg's age and infirmity and Mum drunk. I say I'll come up straightaway. What I see when we arrive makes my blood run cold.

* * *

For some reason, Mum's been trying to light a camping light. It requires a cylinder of pressurized gas to be pushed up underneath and the flame lit. She hasn't put the gas canister in properly but has still pierced the can. She has then struck a match and a ball of flame has shot out. She's wearing a nightdress and it has caught fire. She's managed to pull it off with her hand. When I see it, it sends shivers down my spine.

All that's left is a small lump of molten nylon, the size of a tennis ball. She has left the canister and gone to get some more clothes. You don't need to be a firefighter to see she's been desperately lucky. She's physically fine apart from a large burn on her leg and it could have been much worse. I get some frozen food from the freezer to take the heat out of the burn. She's laid down but won't lie still.

'Mum, you must lie still. I'm trying to deal with your burn.'

'Get off me,' she shouts at the top of her voice, swiping at me with her hand.

I gently push her back down and apply the frozen food. Once the burn starts to look and feel better, she falls asleep. I think that she shouldn't fall asleep downstairs so I wake her up and take her up to bed, covering her with some blankets. Just as I do this, I hear her moan.

'What's up, Mum?' I say, straining to hear what she's asking for.

Again she mumbles inaudibly.

'*I still can't hear you, Mum.*'

She raises her voice further and says three words I thought I'd never hear again.

'*Fuck me, David.*'

15

Down Memory Lane

I instantly recoil. I can't believe my ears.

She says it again. 'Fuck me, David.'

This time, I'm ready with a response to her request: I walk out of the room. I go downstairs. I struggle to speak. I tell Reg that I've put her to bed and to phone me again if there's a problem.

Those three words are flying around inside my head, producing strong emotions. I'm upset and angry that she has asked me again. It also makes me question her actions. She did it when I was alone with her, yet she was only semi-conscious.

How did she know it was just me in the room?

And if she could tell that, did she know what she had been doing to me for all those years when I was growing up?

I leave Mum and Reg and go to the Christmas do. It's a sombre affair for me, with my mind spinning at what I've just seen and heard. Mum's had a lucky escape but she mightn't be so lucky next time. She's drinking heavily again and is an obvious danger to herself and Reg. She has revived bad memories for me. Life is going well for me and I've been able to control what has happened to me as a child to a greater extent. I have never told anyone about our sex contacts and don't see the need. But Mum has managed to destabilize me a little and bring back the insecurities and negativity I thought had gone forever.

In the next few days I think about Mum and how she has badly affected my life in so many ways over so many years and I decide it can't continue. I know she isn't going to change and I then take the biggest decision of my life.

I go to Ludden Vale.

When Mum comes to the door I know that she can instantly see by my face that's something's up, but she doesn't ask me what.

'Let's go and sit down, Mum,' I say. 'I've got something very important to say to you.'

I sit down with Mum and tell her that she will never see or hear from me ever again. She just sits there listening while I talk.

'It's just gone on too long, Mum,' I say, 'and I can't deal with it any more. It's too much for me. It's doing my head in, like it's done for years, but what happened last week, when you practically set fire to yourself and the whole house – it's the last straw. I've had enough of it, Mum.'

I carry on telling her how I can no longer deal with her drinking and the destruction and havoc it has continued to cause in my life – yet now, as always, I find it impossible to mention to her what really went on between us at night when she was drunk.

Mum is still sitting there, listening quietly to what I have to say and she seems very calm about it.

Finally she responds.

'It's OK, David, I know what you're saying. You must do what you have to do. If you change your mind, well you know where I am.'

I give her a hug and then I leave.

It's a huge wrench and I feel absolutely gutted when I look her in the face for the last time and turn and walk away. I have done something I thought I'd never even contemplate, let alone carry out. I have cut my own mother from my life for good. But although I've walked away from her, I'm not so sure she can keep away from me. I assume she'll continue to phone me when she's drunk. But to my complete and utter surprise, she doesn't. I've told her I want nothing more to do with her and, incredibly, she respects and acts on that request. There are no more calls to my house and workplace.

At first, it feels eerie and strange. Whichever way I've turned, Mum has always been there. My earliest memory was of her abusing me as a young child. One of my last memories is of her asking me to fuck her. There have been some fantastic times and I did owe her a huge debt of gratitude for many things. But there have been some desperately bad times and for those I can never forgive her. Now, for the first time in my life, I'm completely free. I feel very strange about it all but I instinctively feel that I've done the right thing.

Yet I'm not happy about it. I can never be. This is my mother and despite her demons and our history, I have never stopped loving her. I miss her but know I can never go back to her. She's my mother but she can't be part of my life. A phone call one night confirms that I've done the right thing.

Mum has had plenty of friends throughout my life but her relationship with them has always came to an abrupt, fatal end. Some of those people have been significant like Reg's daughter and my own grandfather. Once the contact had been broken, it has never been reconnected. Another such person is the receptionist at the vet.

She always has at least half a dozen animals had two dogs, three cats and a tortoise from an early age – so she's still often at the vet's. She's got to know them well and particularly the receptionist. As is Mum's usual practice, she got the woman's number and started phoning her at home. True to form, she started phoning when drunk. Eventually, the receptionist was so cheesed off that she contemplated drastic action and one night she rings me.

'Hiya, I am the receptionist from the vets in Ludden Bridge,' she begins. 'I believe you're Carol Brownstone's son.'

'Yes, I am. What can I do for you?'

'I've been having problems with your mother phoning me at home. I was wondering if you could help.'

This is an unusual phone call to receive but, after all, it isn't surprising. 'Well, I'd love to but unfortunately, I'm now estranged from my mother,' I say. 'We no longer see each other or speak,'

I can sense her anxiety but there's nothing I can do.

'That's a shame. I'm getting to the end of my tether with it now. I'm even contemplating going to the police.'

I can hear the desperation in her voice.

'To be honest, you might end up having to do that,' I reply. 'I don't think that much else is going to stop her.'

I haven't spoken to Mum for some time and have locked all those memories of her away. To hear what she's doing to this poor woman brings it all back into focus. I never hear from the receptionist again and assume that she's sorted it out to her satisfaction. But this incident brings Mum back into my daily thoughts. I really want to go and see her, yet I know I should keep away and continue to do so.

* * *

Turning my back on Mum has been the hardest thing I've ever had to do and feels unnatural. I have learned how to deal with her demands through pacifying her and trying to deal with her. But I know I've had to make a decision that may well shatter her life.

Bringing up her son in challenging circumstances would have been difficult enough. But to see him come to adulthood, go into a successful career and then reject you must be devastating. Every day I think of Mum's pain and want to call her. Reg has stopped phoning too. It means less aggravation but it indicates that he's getting it in the neck as he's the only one left in the house. Despite my lack of emotional connection with him, I fear for his safety.

With no outside support I'm waiting for the day when I see an article in the paper about a bad fire at their house or that Reg had suffered some traumatic and fatal injury. It feels like I'm being melodramatic but I've seen seriously dangerous things happen at their house when she's drunk and as a fireman I know how fragile human life is, so I feel justified in being worried.

I'm not only feeling anxious for both of them but, at this point in my life, despondent about where my own life is heading, and one night my misery and depression come to a head. I don't feel like seeing anyone I know so in spite of my general distaste nowadays for mindless boozing – especially for its own sake – I head for a pub that I would never normally go to and sit in a dark corner, drinking one Coke and Tia Maria after another.

I can no longer make any sense of my life. I have reached a low ebb; I feel lost, abandoned, cut adrift. I have effectively severed connection with the two closest people in life, my mother and my best friend, and now I have no-one I can confide in or rely on, no-one to give me love or support. All my relationships with women seem to come to nothing: they are either one-night stands or, just when they appear to be working out, they come apart at the seams.

I feel as if I too am coming apart at the seams. When I look back at my past, all I can remember is abuse, chaos and violence. When I think about my present life, all I seem to do is walk a dreary treadmill, not just in my job but in my relationships. I have no particular skills apart from those of a fireman, and I'll never be exceptional. For that you need something extra – physical or mental abilities that single you out from the crowd, and I just don't have them.

My relationships always seem to fail, maybe because in my heart of hearts I don't feel I'm good enough, lovable enough, for anyone to want me and love me. The only person who really seemed to love me is Mum, but her love for me is so deeply flawed that, when I think about it, I still feel the same sense of shame and humiliation I did when I was bullied by Karen in my first year at junior school.

When I try to imagine the future, all I can see is more failure, more hopelessness. How can I ever expect to make anything of myself, be more than just an average fire-fighter who will eventually get pensioned off when I'm no longer physically able to do the job? How can I ever expect to find anyone who I can truly love or who will love me, let alone have children with them with whom I would want to play and for whom I could be a real dad?

I have no role model for being a father. I am, deep down, still a child myself, a damaged child, lacking in any feelings of self-worth and any hopes of feeling better, of doing better, of being better. I genuinely do not know at this point why I'm still alive or what I'm still living for.

In this state of deep depression and despair, I return home after the landlord has called for last orders, fix myself one more microwave meal and slump in front of the box. It's a cheesy late-night TV programme and I'm only half watching. I'm about to tune out, turn it off and turn in when I see a man memorize a pack of playing cards in three minutes. Not only does he memorize the whole pack, which seems an astonishing feat in itself, but he also knows where every single card is.

In an instant my mood changes. I have forgotten all about my depression and woes. I think this is cool and that it would be really nice to learn how to do it. I'm intrigued by it. I know it isn't magic and that there must be some kind of mental process involved in it. But as with many things that seem impossible, I assume the guy is a savant, a gifted individual with a special skill.

But that's not me. As Mum would put it, I'm stuck with what I've got.

All the same, I start to wonder. Is that really true? After all, I changed myself physically when I began having karate lessons and then took up long-distance running and finally started working out at the gym. Maybe I could change myself mentally in a similar way. Maybe my memory isn't as bad as I thought it was. Feeling oddly elated, I put all these thoughts to the back of my mind and go to bed.

A few months later, I come across this man in an article in the *Sunday Times*. It says that he has been in northern France playing blackjack, that he uses memory techniques and is self-taught. The article also says that he's written a book. His name is Dominic O'Brien. Not long after this I walk into a bookshop in Leeds and see a pile of memory books on a stand. The one on top is written by Dominic O'Brien. I buy the book, take it home and start reading it.

Within the first few pages, I learn a technique that allows me to recite a list of ten objects forwards and backwards. I'm stunned and think this is magnificent. I know that the book has had a deep impact on me but I can't see a practical use for it so I put it in a cupboard. It languishes there for a few weeks then I decide to have another read. What follows is truly astounding. I learn all the memory techniques in the book and practise them. I find I can do them easily and well. I learn how to memorize a pack of playing cards like Dominic has done on television several months ago, something I would never have thought possible.

I learn how to memorize numbers and can soon memorize a 100-digit number with ease. I use the techniques to memorize capitals of the world: within a short space of time, I can reel them all off. It's now getting scary. I'm performing memory techniques that defy all logic and belief. As I go through the book I add layer upon layer of new techniques and continue to improve my memory ability. Not slowly, like training for a marathon, but quickly. One week I can do a pack of cards in ten minutes, two weeks later I can do it in less than five.

I love the feeling of having an exceptional talent. When I go to work and show them my new party trick of memorizing a pack of cards, they're part bemused, part in awe. Some want to know how to do it and I show them. But no-one's able to match my ability or the speed with which I pick up the techniques. It's slowly dawning on me that I have a gift which is more than just a party trick. I tell some of the boys at work but don't broadcast it. Firefighters are prone to take the mickey at any opportunity and I have one glaring example of this one night.

All the lads on the Watch are watching TV upstairs and I'm downstairs playing around with memorizing cards. I have all the cards laid out on the dining table as I try to work out where every card is. One of the lads comes down to get something out of the kitchen. As he walks behind me, he looks over my shoulder.

'You'll never get anywhere with that shit,' he smirks.

I ignore him and carry on, but underneath I'm annoyed. That's the Fire Service way. If you don't understand something, knock it. Hearing comments like that make me determined to prove him wrong.

There's one area where I can apply my new-found skills at work. I want to see if I can use the memory techniques to pass the promotion exams I previously failed. I take the memory technique for memorizing lists and adapt it for the exam information. The techniques seem to work and information is sticking. Although I worry I might not be able to apply it in the exam, as it approaches I feel more confident. By the time I'm outside the examination hall, instead of being racked with nerves, I'm perfectly calm. Instead of wondering whether I'm going to pass, it's just a question of how high my grade might be.

I sit the exam, answer many of the questions with ease and pass with flying colours. My brain is moving at the speed of light. I'm developing an amazing skill I never knew I had and am applying it in a practical way that is having a substantial impact. Plus, it gives me a whole new level of confidence and self-esteem.

I continue to play around with memory training techniques I've been learning from various memory books, and broadening my knowledge as I come across new and complementary techniques, such as Speed Reading and Mind Mapping.

I'm still making huge strides and am starting to produce results that may even allow me to compete in a memory competition. I've read in various memory books that there's something called the World Memory Championships. I manage to get a list of the results from previous competitions. To my shock and delight, I see that the scores I've been getting at home actually make me a contender: I can consider entering the competition.

I've decided to prepare for the 1996 World Memory Championships in London. I book a train ticket and hotel, the cheapest I can find on the Strand, and in August I go to the competition. It's a life-changing experience for me. The competition is held at Simpson's-in-the-Strand, a traditional London restaurant with a fantastic history, having hosted World Chess Championship competitions in the early 1900s. Over the weekend I compete in the World Memory Championships. The event is a series of 11 different individual disciplines such as the quickest time for a single pack of playing cards and the longest binary digit number I can memorize in half an hour. Out of 11 events I get five top-three finishes and even come second in one. After the first day, I am placed overall third. I'm ecstatic.

I start the second day full of confidence and maintain my third position all day. But during the very last event I make a mistake and drop to fourth. I'm gutted. If someone had offered me fourth place before the start I would have grabbed it with both hands. But after having competed, I rediscover something about myself: I have a fiercely competitive streak and love success.

Another thing happens that weekend: after only eight months of practising memory techniques, I find myself elevated to the position of International Grandmaster of Memory.

* * *

At the time, only three people have achieved the title of International Grandmaster of Memory under competition conditions. I envisaged I might come in the top six or seven but never fourth. After all, this is the World Championships in a field of excellence I've only learned about from a book less than a year before. It's hard for me to take it in.

All my life I have wanted to blend into the wallpaper and not stand out. For the most part, when I have stood out it was for the wrong reasons such as having ginger hair, getting in trouble with the police and not being very good at my job as a firefighter. Sometimes I stood out for positive reasons such as winning the school cross country, but those have been rare occurrences. This is different. Completely off my own bat, I have gone out and taught myself how to do something at an astonishing level. I've discovered the tenacity and drive to push myself onto the world stage.

I've also discovered how to capitalize on my success and promote myself to the media – I contact the *Halifax Evening Courier*, my local paper who interview me and I end up on the front page with a picture of me holding all my medals. I then get in touch with Calendar Television, the regional ITV network, who say they want me to appear on their show. I get nearly six minutes prime airtime, talking about memory, and they test me. I get all the questions right and all the production team seemed genuinely very pleased.

Whatever else I may achieve in the future, this has been a spectacular success. But one thing is always nagging at the back of my mind. Mum. Before our split she knew about the memory stuff and regarded it as a complete waste of time. This surprised me at the time, considering her father had been a well-respected chess player in his own right. What I was doing with the memory was a cerebral exercise in the same way as chess.

But despite her lack of interest when I began doing it, I've just come fourth in the world in this arena and have received media attention as a result. I know she watches a lot of television and that she gets the *Halifax Courier* every day. She must have seen me. I desperately want to phone her and ask her what she thinks. I want her to tell me I've done well. As throughout my life, I want her approval.

But I don't phone her. It makes me sad but I feel that I must remain strong.

* * *

Slowly but surely I've come to terms with Fire Service life and have learnt to stand on my own two feet. I'm now a professional firefighter in every sense of the words. I'm never going to be Firefighter of the Year but I'm competent in every area and very good in some. Working at a busy fire station shows me that I can cope well under extreme pressure. This has come in handy in the memory competition. It's also a surprise as Mum is the exact opposite, unable to deal with the mildest of stressful situations.

I've developed a liking for training, having been on several courses where I've learnt information that I've taught to all the watches on station. I like delivering the material, teaching something new to people. The station is run by a guy called John Winton. I know nothing about him personally other than he's my Station Commander. He has a reputation for being firm but fair, usually erring on the side of the lads on station when it came to disputes and problems. He was well liked and any contact I had previously had with him had been very positive.

After the competition he pulls me to one side and asks if I can help him. This is a little unusual as I don't expect an officer of his rank to be asking me, a bottom-rank firefighter, for assistance. But Johnny is above petty things such as rank. He says he's struggling with a Health & Safety exam where there's a 50% failure rate. He wants to know if I can help him memorize the huge quantity of information required to pass the exam.

He shows me the text and I help him Mind Map one page. I take the book home and Mind Map 20 pages that night. In the morning I show him what I'd done and he can do the same for the rest of the book. He's suitably impressed and used Mind Mapping for all his material. It's a brilliant success and he passes with flying colours.

Teaching Johnny is a turning point. He shows me there's a true value in what I know, that people in the real world can practically apply my methods. This is really exciting and is slowly leading me towards a new direction in my life.

* * *

I meet Alison one night in a pub. She is tall, vivacious, funny and direct, and she has two children. I've made a connection with her that I've never made with anyone else and, a week later, she moves in with me.

This all happens a week before Christmas 1996. I help Ally prepare and wrap presents for her two kids, Corinne, 13, and Matthew, 5, and we all sit around together on Christmas Day morning opening them. I've never been near children before and have always actively avoided them. I feel out of my depth with Cori and Matt, but they're quick to accept me. I know I want to be with Ally. That Christmas shows me what it can be like in a good relationship.

* * *

In 1997 I come third overall in the Memory Championships and in April 1998 I achieve the unthinkable: I perfectly recite 22,500 digits of the mathematical formula *Pi* to set a new Guinness record. Yet in the midst of all this, I am really only wondering about one thing.

Does Mum know about my new success? I desperately want to share it with her. And so I take the second biggest decision of my life.

16

Sparks and Embers

*B*y the beginning of 1999 my life has turned around in a way I couldn't possibly have imagined when I was sitting in the dark corner of that pub feeling sorry for myself while I drank Cokes and Tia Marias only a few years ago.

I'm now a *Guinness Book of Records* memory record-holder, World Memory Championships medallist and International Grandmaster of Memory. The media continue to show interest and I'm doing a steady flow of television, radio, magazine and newspaper interviews. I have also been training senior fire officers in memory skills and while still working in the Fire Service have started a new career as a motivational speaker.

Ally and I get on well and she's very supportive of my new career. I have now been living with her and the kids for two years. Cori had turned fifteen and is a great teenager – quiet, shy, serious and very pretty. We have built a wonderful bond through mutual trust and respect, and play a significant part in each other's lives. She still sees her father regularly, which is really cool. She calls me David but treats me like a stepfather.

My relationship with Matt is just as good but different. He is almost the opposite of Cori, full of himself with a cheeky smile and short mousy hair. He hasn't seen his natural father since he was two and he's just turned seven. It takes Matt and me a while to realize something but when we do it's a magical experience – that I want to be his dad and he wants to be my son. Matt and I have slowly but surely built a father–son relationship. We love each other as if we'd been together since the day he was born. I love everything about him. He's the boy I always wanted to be – socially intelligent, a good mixer with other kids, popular, interested and with a razorlike wit. I worship the ground he walks on.

I've come to feel that being a parent to both Cori and Matt is a true gift. It's the best feeling in the world. Because of this, I realize that Mum must be hurting really badly. She brought me up virtually single-handed. She has deep-rooted problems that have made her do unspeakable things but I still believe that she didn't know that she had done them come the morning.

I talk to Ally about Mum, though I don't tell her about the sexual abuse. I talk about the drinking and how bad it was; about the sleepless nights when I was a kid and the violence. I go through the reasons I've turned my back on her. I tell Ally how much I miss Mum and how much I want to know that she's alright. Ally suggests that I consider getting in touch if it means that much to me.

* * *

I think about it very hard before I make the call. And even after making the decision I leave it some time before I do it. I speak to her by telephone first. Ally is by my side when I make the call.

'Are you OK?' she asks, holding my hand.

'I'm fine,' I reply.

She gives me the phone and I dial the number.

My mother answers the phone. 'Hello,' she says.

'Hiya Mum, it's David,' I say quietly.

She goes silent and doesn't say a thing.

'I was wondering if I could come up and see you.'

She still doesn't say anything. She has never been so quiet. I am half expecting her to drop the phone and have the shortest conversation we've ever had, but eventually she speaks.

'Yes, of course. When were you thinking of?'

We have a brief conversation about when would be the best time for me to come and we hang up. I come off the phone feeling shell-shocked.

There have been no histrionics, crying, shouting or accusations. It's been an entirely civil conversation. We have arranged for me to go and see her in a very rational, simple way. It is good but strange.

A few days later I go to see my mother.

* * *

I knock on the door and she answers it. She looks a little unsure about what to do, just as I am. Without any hugging or kissing, I go into the middle room.

Reg is sitting there in his chair. It takes me by surprise, not because he's there but because of how he looks. He's now 89 and looks every one of those years. His eyes are sunken hollows in his head and he's very thin. Even five years ago he was in pretty good shape but now he truly is an old man.

'Hiya, Reg,' I say, not sure whether to say anything more.

He looks up as if he hasn't expected to see me. 'Oh, hello, David,' he replies.

I sit down with Mum at the dining table and chat with her. I tell her everything about the memory championships, public speaking, Ally, the kids and the Fire Service.

She listens intently. I can tell she's making a real effort. Mum has never been a very good listener, sometimes showing no interest in you at all. But now she wants to know. I ask her how she is and Reg too. She says everything is as it's always been which I can see is true. The house looks exactly the same – she even has the same pets. We agree that she and Reg should come to the house and meet Ally and the kids. I leave, feeling I've made the right decision. Only time will tell if that is to be the case or if the havoc I know she's capable of creating will come back and haunt me again.

Once home, I tell Ally and the kids about Mum and what's happened. It isn't long before they come up to the house and meet Mum and Reg. Everything goes really well and it seems like Mum is a different person. From then on, we have regular contact. Between the times I see her, she never phones the house. I won't put up with it. I'm petrified that Matt will pick up the phone and she'll be drunk, but she never phones when she's had a drink. Not once.

As always, we never discuss the drinking. I have no idea if she's doing it and, if so, how much. It has always been the great unspoken subject between us and even now it remains so. But we both know. She knows her drinking has split us up once before. And I know she wants to handle it her way and that there's nothing I would be able to do about it. The unspoken rule is that I'm not to question her about her drinking and she isn't to phone me when she's drunk. This time, she keeps to it.

Then, on 16 February 1999, within two months of getting back in touch with her, something happens that I think may send Mum over the edge.

Reg dies.

* * *

He hasn't died of anything to do with Mum or her drinking, but of old age. He has been very feeble for the short time I've been back in his life. Of course, it hits her like a tank going down a hill. She is devastated beyond comprehension. Reg's dying leaves a hole in her heart and her life that will never be filled again.

After Reg's death, Mum is a different person. She seems to have lost all sense of purpose and will to live. I know I have to keep a close eye on her and make her feel part of my family. She needs a constant connection with the outside world. I speak to her every day to see how she is. She doesn't have much to say but is happy to listen to what's happening in my busy life, whether it's memory or work or the kids. I go to see her at least once a week and take her out places, sometimes with Ally and the kids. We go to Liverpool and round the docks. She enjoys the fresh air and the walk.

One day I take her to the indoor market in Halifax. She has mentioned that she needs a new jacket so we buy her one. It's quite cheap but decent quality. On receiving it, she bursts into tears in the middle of the market. She is so used to buying things secondhand and I can never remember a time when she's done it differently. It gives me such a lot of pleasure to be there for her, taking her for meals and buying her things.

During the second half of 1999 I feel closer to her. We chat about things, although never about her drinking. She is really interested in my memory training, so I get her a full-size copy of my *Guinness Book of Records* memory record certificate, have it framed and give it to her. It takes pride of place in the middle room above the fireplace.

She spends time with a friend of hers, Laura, who is about the same age as Mum and whose two boys are a similar age to me at school. They go to the Halifax Playhouse together and Mum speaks to me about these trips in the fondest terms. She has a pact with Laura, who knows about her drinking but, quite rightly, isn't prepared for it to be an issue when they go to see the plays. Mum never drinks when they go out together. Despite having destroyed many relationships with people close to her, she respects Laura's wish and honours her request.

She also has a friend called Ted. I don't know how they've met but he definitely knows about her problems. She likes him and they do things together. There's no romantic inclination at all and they're good for each other. I like the fact that she has friends to spend time with apart from me. It appears that against all odds and at an unlikely stage in her life, Mum has changed.

But one night when Ally and I have been out drinking, we start having a row about our relationship and some difficulties we've been going through. Ally has been pushing me hard for me to talk more deeply and honestly about myself than I have ever done before with anyone.

Then I blurt it out.

'My mother abused me.'

Ally just looks at me stunned.

I start mentioning what happened to me as a child but then I shut up. The alcohol has created something in me which has made me want to share this information for the first time with anyone in 26 years but I can't bring myself to say too much. With us both drunk and me clamming up, the conversation quickly moves on to something else.

In the morning, we discuss it again now that we're sober. I revert to type, not wanting to talk about it. I feel that I've let something slip that should never have come out. It's my secret and mine alone; I have been almost proud of my ability to keep it locked away and deal with it on my terms. I'm also sure, even at this stage, that Mum still doesn't know what she did all those years ago. This is my very own secret that absolutely no-one else has known about.

But not any more.

Ally says that her concern, aside from the problem it may have caused me by not dealing with this most sensitive of issues, is Matt. We agree that it's best that he doesn't spend time alone with Mum.

I'm still afraid that Mum might find out. We have a stable relationship that works on both sides. But that fragile situation would be smashed apart if she were to be told, even if it's an unintentional slip of the tongue. I have been adept at keeping this most incredible of personal information to myself. I have done so for nearly 30 years. I trust Ally absolutely not to say anything to Mum but at the same time in the back of my mind, I worry that one of us might let it slip. The consequences of Mum finding out are just too awful for me to contemplate.

* * *

A month before Christmas I get a phone call from a fellow memory man who wants me to set up a dotcom business in the learning field. He and his boss would provide the seed money and I would run it, hire the staff, get the website built and make it all come together. More than this, I would do it full-time and receive a wage.

After meeting them and talking it through with Ally, I decide to take the job. I then go in to work and ask for a year's sabbatical. They agree to it and a few weeks later, just before Christmas, I effectively leave the Fire Service, having spent eleven years as an operational firefighter. I have worked on seven watches on five fire stations with over a hundred men. I joined the Fire Service a young lad with no idea about life. I leave it a confident man, comfortable in his own skin, with a bag full of experiences behind him.

During those eleven years I've also learnt how to cope with being woken up by a very bright light when I was fast asleep and have thereby been able to turn around a horrifying experience that haunted and blighted my childhood.

It's truly the end of an era.

* * *

Christmas is a joyous occasion. We cook dinner at our house and have a table full of people to share it with.

Johnny, my former Station Commander, is now a close friend and he's there. Ally's best mate's there too. So is Mum.

Life couldn't be better. I have my family round me. Matt is now my son in every real sense of the word and I loved Cori like a daughter. Ally and I are getting on really well and I have a new job with a good wage and fantastic prospects. Mum is stable and we've developed a strong relationship based on trust and respect. For the first time in my life, I have arrived at a place where I feel happy, relaxed and good about myself.

In 2000 I become MD of an Internet company, working in areas for which I have a deep passion – learning and memory. I see Mum and speak to her regularly. Sometimes she's chatty and sometimes happy just to listen. I go with the flow. But most important, she appears stable and there are no more drunken incidents that I know about, which is great news to me.

On Saturday, 18 March 2000 I book tickets for Ally, the kids and me to see a concert in Bradford. In the interval I ring Mum but there's no reply. The following day, we've planned a family day in Blackpool and are going to take Mum with us. But I still can't get hold of her and assume she must be feeling a bit rough. When by the evening, I've not heard anything from Mum, I decide to go to the house.

* * *

Ally comes with me. As we approach, I notice the lights are on, which isn't unusual and lifts my mood immediately.

'Look, Ally, all the lights are on. That means she's been drinking. She must be in the house.'

I knock but there's no answer. I try the door handle and it's open. I gently push the door and step into the hallway.

'Mum,' I call out several times but am met with silence.

We go into the middle room. Timmy, the dog, and the cats are there. Timmy's pleased to see me. He's always like this as I often walk him when I go for visits.

Ally goes into the kitchen and I follow her in. Everything's normal. I know now that Mum is drunk and asleep in bed. We check the gas cooker. My eternal worry is that she will leave the gas on and blow up the house. Then we both go upstairs. Ally walks into the middle room. Even though there's now no bed in there, Mum may have passed out on the floor. I've known her do this all over the house when I lived at home.

She isn't in that room, so I check in my old bedroom. As I open the door, a rush of memories comes flooding back. The bed and bedclothes are the same as I used nearly fifteen years before. I remember the shouting, the violence, my mother trying to rape me and me shivering in the corner of the room while she pleaded with me to have sex with her.

I shake myself out of it.

With Ally at my side I walk along the small landing towards the last bedroom. Her door is open and we go in.

My mother is lying on her bed. She is half naked, wearing nothing but a threadbare jumper, her legs covered in bruises where she used to fall down the stone steps of the house every time she had been drinking. She has her hand inside her jumper as if clutching her heart.

I go to wake her up, but then I realize there's no point. She has passed away.

Epilogue

Just before the funeral I have an open coffin in an anteroom. Cori and Matt come to the service and I tell them they can go in the room if they wish to. I tell everyone else they can do the same.

When those that want to see her have done so, I go in on my own. Considering the dreadful state I found her in, she now seems completely different after she has been prepared. She looks serene and peaceful.

I don't cry at all, yet I feel an astonishing array of emotions.

Bitterness that she has been snatched away from me when it has only been fifteen months since we've been reunited.

Guilt that I was out enjoying myself the night before while my mother was dying alone; guilt that I was out all day having fun while her body was rotting away on her bed at home.

Gratitude that she has died the way she did. I had always feared that she might die of cancer, because there was a history of it on her side of the family. A relatively quick and sudden death with no gradual decline is a blessing. It could have been much worse.

But I'm also feeling confused.

Why was I the one to find her dead when it was obviously going to have the biggest impact on me? If I had been on holiday or away on business, then I wouldn't have had to see her in such a dreadful state.

All these emotions conspire to make me feel I'm walking a tightrope. I feel fine one minute, out of control the next. My mother has taken herself to the edge of the cliff and has finally thrown herself off it.

I feel as though I'm chained to her as she falls and that she's going to take me with her. But she hasn't, because I won't let her.

My mother had an addictive personality. Her weakness was alcohol. I too have an addictive personality, but it's up to me to decide how to use it. I have discovered a way to channel my compulsions in a positive way and am enjoying a quality of life I hadn't even known existed five years before and it's too precious to throw away. My mother may have thrown herself off that cliff but I'm not going with her.

I also feel a poignant kind of relief that she has passed away. It is an unsettling, disturbing emotion but I know that since Reg's death she has been merely existing. She needed more than that and she wasn't getting it. I did my best, but my best just wasn't enough. Through death she has eventually achieved the peace she never found in life. But the questions are echoing in the back of my mind.

Why, Mum? Tell me why. Why did you do all those awful things to me? Why did you always act as if nothing had happened in the morning? Did you ever remember anything at all? When you came to me at night did you have any idea of what you were doing? And why me, not Reg? Why did you let all the questions pile up and never give me any answers?

I have always hoped that one day I'd have answers but now I know this will never happen. I have to let go, I have to move on. Standing there, looking at my mother, a sense of peace comes to me for the first time in my life. I realize I no longer need to *know or understand what went on and why. It is in the past now, as she is now in mine. It's over. The past cannot be altered but it can be gently extinguished, like a once raging fire that has been brought under control and can finally be allowed to dwindle right down into a pile of ashes. As I look at my mother for one last time, I release us both from the grip of the past.*

It opens up gently for me, like the nuts on the bolts of Dad's motorbike, which he told me not to screw too tightly, but just enough to allow them to be loosened again if need be; like the brakes that I released just as Reg taught me in those far off days when he was still kind; like the pod of peas bursting from their shells when I sat with my mother all those years ago until I left her there on her own, in her garden.

It weeps gently to me, and all the pain and heartache inside breaks into tiny little pieces, releasing all my unanswered questions.

I gaze at my mother for as long as I can, then lean over her body.

'Goodbye, Mum,' I whisper.

I turn and leave the room, and I never see my mother again.

Acknowledgements

I would like to thank the following people for making this book possible: Richard McCann, Sally Potter, Angela McCulloch, Julie Holdsworth, Elizabeth Salmon, Rema and David Sim, Paul McGee, Marc Woods, James Snowdon, Elizabeth Clark. And finally, special thanks to Martin Noble for his fantastic edit and bringing my story to life.